Praise for *Leadership Power*

Peter J. Daniels's book, *Leadership Power*, should be required reading for anyone who has a position of leadership in business or in the Church. As I devoured this book, I was amazed by Peter's ability to communicate. I was also transfixed by the wealth of truth, insight, and wisdom in this book—treasures that have the power to benefit each of our lives. It has taken Peter's lifetime to compile this wisdom through his experience and study of the Word. Now we can so easily glean from his insights by reading this book and putting the principles he presents into practice. I cannot give a sufficiently high recommendation for this amazing book! Get it, read it, and apply it to your life. As you do, I believe you will see a huge increase in your abilities and effectiveness as a leader.

—Rick Renner
Author, Pastor, Church Founder, and T.V. Broadcaster

Dr. Peter J. Daniels writes from a never-ending plethora of successful experiences. He still maintains the dynamism of youth and the insights of age. Read and reread this magnificent volume. You'll add a powerful dimension to your life.

—Dr. John Edmund Haggai
Founder of Haggai International

Thank you, Peter J. Daniels, for writing this engaging book on true leadership power. More than just theories, your wise words of experience challenge every one of us to be pragmatic, skilled, and steadfast. Now more than ever in history we need a book like this.

—John Mason
President of Insight International/Insight Publishing Group
Author of *An Enemy Called Average*
and numerous other bestselling books.

Once again, Peter J. Daniels brings his energy and vast experience to the desperately important issue of leadership. From the individual's initial inklings of leadership through to one's destiny, the plan and process that Daniels presents is infused with the practicalities and power of commitment.

—Dr. D. S. Reimer
Winnipeg, Canada

The first time I met Peter J. Daniels he impressed me greatly and now it is my honour to write a short endorsement for his new book, *Leadership Power.* Daniels writes with passion, authority, and from a lifetime of experience—anyone who sees themselves as leader, or future leader, needs to read it. This book certainly challenged me... there is just so much great material in this book, especially for young people. In Chapter 5 Peter deals with making and setting goals 'The Goals Formula'—that information alone is gold! I will certainly be getting copies of *Leadership Power* for my grandsons.

—Dr. Colin Stringer
Author of *The 800 Horsemen*
Queensland, Australia

Peter J. Daniels has masterfully crafted every word to inspire, challenge, and uplift any generation. This book will supercharge its reader to take up the leadership role and walk in their divine destiny.

—Chris Greenwood, a.k.a. Manafest

Everybody has leadership capacity and responsibility. It can be a difficult concept to quantify, tricky to nail down, and at times slippery to get a grip on. Peter J. Daniels insights in this book will get you to bedrock understanding. You will be left in no doubt as to what is needed. A clarity will come as to how to build leadership power. Daniels is qualified to impart wisdom on this subject. If you are ready to be challenged again, this book will stir the "leader" in you.

—Bill Nott
Pastor at Liberty Life Church in South Australia

The art of authentic leadership, in the modern and turbulent world we live in, has become a real big crisis. It takes a man who can bridge the present and the wisdom of the last generations in a practical and knowledgeable fashion.

Peter J. Daniels has brilliantly shared in this book, great treasures, especially for those who aspire to be great leaders in any sphere of society.

Leadership Power is rich with practical knowledge and ideas that have been tested and proven. Daniels's way of presenting the leadership crisis and showing steps of resolving it is very strategic. It is powerful enough to re-establish the already established and raise the aspiring, on any level of the leadership ladder, to new highs.

I recommend everybody read, ponder through, and apply the vast knowledge and principles provided in this book. We need powerful leaders in this day and hour. With no authentic leaders the world goes to war with itself.

—Henry Madava
Senior Pastor, Victory Christian Churches Ukraine
President of Christ for All Cities International Ministries
President of Peace and Wellbeing Charitable Fund

At 80 years and 7 months I read the manuscript you sent me, *Leadership Power: Beyond the Smoke and Mirrors.* In my 20s, it would have been a book of great ideas for leaders; at my present age, I see it as a book of great truth. Strangely, until the fourth quarter of life, time is cheap. At my age I now know that the currency of the universe is time, when it is spent, your wage will be paid, the real cost will be known! Will it be well done or saved yet so by fire? The book is splendid.

—Dr. John Avanzini
God's Outreach, Inc. in Fort Worth, TX

Peter J. Daniels has always struck me as being an extremely wise man on a mission. As an octogenarian who has moved from humble beginnings to the top of the business world with minimal formal education, he is worth listening to.

I have always been intrigued by his way of thinking and how that influences his approach to business, his relationships and interaction with economies, and fiscal policies worldwide.

His latest literary offering leaves the reader with no illusions as to how he transacts business, which in the main challenges the norms and sets him apart, and makes him a cut above the rest in his sphere of influence.

I find his style refreshing even though—as he takes time to point out—there is no gain without pain, but the Bible—which is one of the main sources of inspiration for all he has accomplished—is replete with examples of characters he has emulated in his rise to the top.

This book is a manual not just for getting to the top, more importantly it highlights the character & skills you need to remain at the top perpetually.

I wholeheartedly recommend this book to anyone aspiring to make their mark in a sphere of influence and leave a mark as indelible as Daniels will when God calls him home.

Enjoy the read!

—Dr. Sola Fola-Alade
Lead Pastor of The Liberty Church in London, England

Leadership Power: Beyond Smoke and Mirrors is so simple that one must have help to misunderstand it! But, then it is written by a colorblind, dyslectic, once-illiterate bricklayer who educated himself to become the best platform speaker in the world. His accomplishments in business are legendary, and now at 85 he has given us another opportunity to sit at his feet and learn. I have been blessed to know this bricklayer - statesman for many years. Any book he has written is a must read for all who are willing to be honest with themselves and with God, those who really benefit mankind through his or her leadership. This one is the best of the stack. If this is your first Peter J. Daniels book, start with his own story and don't quit until you've read everything he has written. If you're a quitter, read this one first and fix that, and then you're on your way to a life, or rather a journey worth living.

—Pastor Kenneth Copeland
Kenneth Copeland Ministries

Peter J. Daniels's book on leadership is like cement when added to sand, gravel and water, makes concrete. This book is like concrete poured and placed into a well-formed structure. The defined leadership principles laid out in this writing, when actively applied into real life situations, bring strength, encouragement, and a solid foundation for business and life. These principles are pragmatic, not theoretical, and laid out with a clear path to follow. He is able to put into words what every successful entrepreneur needs to understand in life. I have found these standards true in my own life experiences.

—Mark Dorazio
President of Dorazio Enterprises, Inc. in Austin, TX

There are few moments in one's lifetime where one is able to view the accurate explanation of one of life's challenges. *Leadership*

Power is one of those times. In it, Peter J. Daniels unpacks leadership, its power and pitfalls, right before our eyes. Having walked along side this extraordinary man, I have discovered the depth and accuracy by which he has lived, loved, and led.

The unveiling of the difference between being a manager and a leader will transform your thinking about leadership altogether. Once again all one can say is bravo Peter, you penned the thoughts that have been hidden so long in this exemplary work.

—Dr. Robb Thompson
Pastor, Speaker, and Businessman

Leaders are seldom those who most people perceive them to be. Leadership is rarely what the majority understand it as it really is.

In Estonia, brave generals and uncompromising national politicians gave their lives as a result of the ruthless Communist aggression which enslaved our nation for years. Yet during it's darkest, most difficult years, poets, song writers, musicians, and conductors kept a nation's spirit alive as they lead subtly, unwaveringly, through music and song. Who are the real leaders of today? Peter J. Daniels is one of those leaders, who in this book—with years of experience—takes a serious, honest, practical, and straightforward look at leaders and leadership, asking penetrating convicting questions while at the same time giving practical timely advice. All this from Mr. Daniels, for whom I have nothing but respect and gratitude!

—Bishop Märt Vähi
Estonian Christian Pentecostal Church
Co-Founder of Village of Hope in Estonia
National Recipient of the Order of the Red Cross

PETER J. DANIELS

Author | Entrepreneur | Philanthropist | Speaker

LEADERSHIP POWER

Beyond Smoke and Mirrors

LEADERSHIP POWER

Requests for further information: peterjdaniels@peterjdaniels.com
Website: www.wces.vu

ISBN: 978-1-4866-1549-0

Word Alive Press
131 Cordite Road, Winnipeg, MB R3W 1S1
www.wordalivepress.ca

WORD ALIVE
—PRESS—

Cataloguing in Publication may be obtained through Library and Archives Canada

Other books by the same author:

How to Be Happy Though Rich
How to Reach Your Life Goals
How to Handle a Major Crisis
How to Be Motivated All the Time
How to Have the Awesome Power of Public Speaking
Miss Phillips, You Were Wrong
Destiny of the 3rd Millennium (comprehensive tutorial)
How to Create Your Own Dynamic Mission Statement that Works
Global Survey into Multi-Level Marketing
Living on the Edge (autobiography)
Leadership Power
A Christian Code of Conduct... The Missing Link
Willpower: The Integrity of the Soul
The Way I See It (Graham K. Daniels)

Dedicated to:
All the followers who make leadership possible.

CONTENTS

PREFACE

Many books on leadership can appear to be masterpieces but are authored by theoreticians who have never led anything significant and have surmised and guessed their way to faulty conclusions. To understand the peculiarities and actions of those that have leadership power and to explain it in a meaningful way, an author must first have felt the hot fires of absolute responsibility and the weight and turmoil of possible catastrophe ... to have mentally, physically, and emotionally felt the pain. Theory may be the language of the scholar, but pragmatism is the language of the leader.

We are now experiencing a world of make-believe that has permeated the corridors of international relations, politics, media, and religion. The art of compromise has created many faces that circumnavigate what is right, substituting it with what can be gotten away with. The two questions that must be asked are:

1. Do we have the skilled leadership necessary to guide us in this the early part of the twenty-first century?
2. Are we prepared to accept the adjustments required to acquire safety and prosperity?

We are living in a dangerous and unpredictable world. We continue to drift toward unimaginable horrors by ignoring the unheeded warning signals of the past.

Circumstances may catapult us into nuclear war, or unstoppable superbugs may spread in plague proportions after escaping from scientific experimental laboratories. The possibility of complete and utter financial collapse of banks and financial institutions, bringing galloping deflation, could destroy all agricultural and food processing. A computer shutdown would bring everything to a halt within seconds. The human needs of starving and persecuted people by mass uncontrolled migration may dissolve national borders that could obliterate the civilized structure of many nations, or ignorant indifference could destroy us from within.

The need for leadership is now! It is up to individuals to accept personal responsibility— first for themselves, secondly for their family, and thirdly for their country.

Throughout the long history of humankind, there have always been those selfless beings who, ignoring all opposition, allowed their lives to represent more than their own existence. In doing so, they have stood strong against poverty, injustice, and ignorance. These giants of the human race have provided strength to the weak, wisdom to counter misunderstanding, help to the poor, and relief to the sick and oppressed. Their radiant lives shine brightly against a darkening world and confirm God's presence wherever and whenever confusion and vacillation impede progress. The presence of these individuals can escape recognition in the sameness of everyday life. They are seen to rise to occasions of urgency, opportunity, and need. At such times, they stand supreme and are called leaders.

God has some special things to say concerning the mantle of leadership: "*Behold I have given him for a witness to the people, a leader and commander to the people*" (Isaiah 55:4); "*He that ruleth over men must be just, ruling in the fear of God*" (2 Samuel 23:3).

Alexander the Great said, "I am not afraid of an army of lions led by a sheep; I am afraid of an army of sheep led by a lion."

1

FACE THE FACTS

The door of a great age of history is about to close, and only a flickering light of hope remains, struggling to pierce the dark clouds of the false confidence proclaimed by indecisive, corrupt leaders. The eternal scales of balance have already proclaimed their grim verdict, and the pendulum of destiny has swung its long arm toward the possible obliteration of the whole human race.

The shameful chronicles of the nineteenth, twentieth, and now the twenty-first century are yet to unfold their grim, unstoppable consequences. These will continue to haunt the global population as it plays out many of its pent-up desires in reactionary events. Confidence in the usefulness of the United Nations has long since gone. It has lost all credibility and is now administered by a teeming mass of puffed-up, incompetent puppet-bureaucrats who have been jobbed into office, seduced by the vain prestigious possibility of a grandstand seat at their well-publicised conferences. In reality, the major decisions have already been made by powerful lobby groups plotting behind closed doors. We can no longer depend on the United Nations to guide us, as was the hope when it was created. At that time, then President of the United States of America, Theodore Roosevelt, proclaimed four essential human freedoms: the freedom of speech and expression, the freedom of worship, the freedom from want, and the freedom from fear. These have long since been forgotten.

The United Nations's meetings have become more expensive and theatrical, without any real positive enforceable outcomes in relation to the problems they are supposed to solve. The question must be asked: Who is really behind the curtain setting the agenda? It would seem to the most casual observer—and the evidence is clear for all to see—that those involved all appear to be unfit for the high offices they occupy. Gunboat diplomacy, once used in the past by powerful nations to get agreements with smaller countries on unwanted deals, is now replaced by bribes and large gifts to swing the voting power. It all seems to be an exercise in a shabby undercover auction where the prize goes to the highest bidder and to hell with the consequences! Who cares anyway?

Winston Churchill's remarks at the commencement of the United Nations have proved to be prophetic. He said, "We must be sure that its work is fruitful, that it is a reality and not a sham, that it is a force for action and not merely a frothing of words, that it is the true temple of peace in which the shields of many nations can someday be hung, and not merely a cockpit in the Tower of Babel."[1] Over the last one hundred years, we have endured two major world wars, many military conflicts, and bullying by harsh dictatorships that have inflicted acts of savagery, slavery, and greed on innocent people. These were nurtured at the roots by the glorification of war and power by monarchs, marauding tribes, and ambitious and glory-seeking military and political leaders.

Unfortunately, the vibrations of war, power, fame, and territorial expansion continue. We now have before us a new, rich,

---

1 "The Sinews of Peace ('Iron Curtain Speech')," *Winston Churchill.org*, March 5, 1946, https://www.winstonchurchill.org/resources/speeches/1946-1963-elder-statesman/the-sinews-of-peace.

global target called "market supremacy." This has become the irresistible, unquenchable, uncontrollable aphrodisiac that continues to be stimulated and encouraged by demanding and dissatisfied populations of many countries with no understanding of the realities of personal obligation, responsibility, and economics. It appears that despite the obvious benefits of democracy, this has now become a demanding, hostile monster that has failed the thrifty and honest citizen with tax hikes in order to support the careless, undisciplined part of the populace who continue to milk the system, increasing the burden on others in the community.

In many countries, most people, believing in what they call the "right of entitlement," are demanding a larger piece of the expanding economic pie, somehow imagining that it still exists. They blame their governments for non-delivery and continually accuse the commercial world of greed.

There is an urgent need for capable, progressive, strong leadership in all areas of society throughout the world. Some nations—that for decades have sought handouts because of bad government structures and unwillingness to develop their own—resources will finally be forced to become self-reliant. This may produce some new forms of government with transparent checks, balances, and boundaries, as well as harsh, automatically enforceable penalties for non-compliance. People in many nations are gasping for leadership with a voice of integrity and reason, overlooking the fact that the great pool of humanity is comprised of imperfect beings.

> **THE POWER TO ENFORCE IS PART OF LEADERSHIP, BECAUSE WITHOUT POWER, LEADERSHIP IS USUALLY REDUCED TO MANAGEMENT OR MERELY INFLUENCE.**

What is often not understood is that leadership, and the power associated with it, have seduced men and women down through the ages. The power to enforce is part of leadership, because without power, leadership is usually reduced to management or merely influence. The great Lord Acton summed it up in clear and concise language when he said, "Power tends to corrupt, and absolute power corrupts absolutely." Leaders must decide whether the end result justifies or determines the means.

We have come to believe a fallacy that goes against the facts of history: to be a successful leader, you must adopt some irrefutable personal qualities to succeed. In my fifty year study of history, I have seen every one of those so-called virtues discarded in whole—or in part—by individuals who nevertheless became great leaders.

The least talked about are biblical leaders like Moses, probably the greatest leader of all time, who welded a nation together that still exists today. Moses killed a man, was quick-tempered, and disobeyed God. When he was told to speak to a rock to get water, he struck the rock in a fit of anger, and paid the penalty of not being able to enter the Promised Land. Judah had several wives, yet he committed adultery with a harlot. King David was a liar, sexual predator, and pre-meditated murderer. Abraham lied about his wife to protect himself. Samson was blessed with special gifts, but he was infatuated with sex. Peter the apostle was an angry liar, and Paul killed and persecuted Christians. Nevertheless, all of them became great leaders. Some, in defence, may point to other more honorable biblical figures, such as Joseph, Nehemiah, and Daniel, but they were managers who worked under the mandate of a king's sovereign jurisdiction.

In the early stages of the twenty-first century, the Christian church globally has never had so many conferences on leadership, yet it has never seen such an absence of real leaders. In general, the Christian church teaches and propagates a strange kind of leadership—which is really subservient management—with little or no understanding that executive leadership can be taken as well as given. Subservient leadership occurs in a business or a philanthropic group when the board of directors chooses a president who may have to juggle decisions to satisfy one or more powerful board members, thereby becoming subservient.

We do not see the totality of authority of the leader who stands alone on a personally constructed noble cause. A manager with nothing to manage becomes nothing, but leaders, because of their persona and aura even without power, can still attract a following. The reality is a mishmash of the world in which we live. There will always be a mine-field of activity involving crises, change, and power struggles that operates according to rules based on the simple need to survive.

We also tend to overlook the personality, moods, and private priorities of the leader, which often hide the dark truth buried in the silence of his own mind. However, we know full well that the story told to followers and the public may require some adjustment and camouflage before presentation. Leaders—although strangely gifted—are still imperfect human beings, and once they have sipped the cup of power, change is inevitable.

As we turn the pages of modern and ancient history, we are confronted with the many strange and powerful happenings of change—things built, created, or destroyed by fools, geniuses, saints, or psychopaths. Then by chance, we stumble across the few who were honorable, great, and compassionate.

There are many stories of causes and events, and individuals who have won or lost empires. In some cases, we have accepted as fact silly fictitious folk heroes like Saint George of "Saint George and the Dragon." As the saying goes, "If all you seek as a leader is glory, then you may envy Napoleon Bonaparte, but Napoleon envied Caesar, and Caesar envied Alexander the Great, and Alexander the great envied Hercules, who never existed!"

We often refer to the records of history to obtain clarity and find them wanting, because they are usually recorded and tampered with by the victors under the demands of the all-powerful hero, who—full of vanity and self-aggrandizement—has often embellished the story.

I believe it is fatuous academic recklessness to assess and come to a conclusion about the results achieved by leaders without relating to the humanity of these people who have shaped the world in which we live. We must ask the questions: What type of people were they? How and what awakened them? What was it that reshaped their persona and exposed their strength and secret weaknesses at the awakening of what we call "leadership power?"

We all understand that power, glory, wealth, and fame—when bestowed on any individual—can release and unveil many previously well-hidden and complicated desires. History records for us cowards, heroes, despots, dictators, saints, and benefactors, all of whom were endowed with the mysterious title of "leader." I have known and worked with some of them and discovered them to be finicky, proud, arrogant, self-opinionated, and greedy—geniuses who are always highly motivated and imbued with visions of grandeur. They have transitional friendships and flexible loyalties with secret, unwritten agendas. They are people-users and change relationships to suit their needs. When people are no longer useful to them, they discard them like rag dolls.

Climbing the leadership ladder, they look into the future and use their imagination to create what they want it to become. As skillful, ambitious opportunists, they gravitate towards those they can use or who can assist them at any given time. They possess enormous charm and motivate by persuasion and fear—which they can use at will with prodigious emotional energy—and they have the uncanny ability to know exactly when to use these attributes in correct measure to obtain the desired results.

Behind closed doors, they develop schemes and plans, holding urgent secret meetings in bathrooms and by sneaky whispering in corridors. They selectively choose individuals they have groomed to be loyal through trickery and manipulation to do their dirty work for them. Under the guise of a mighty cause and by their almost hypnotic overpowering presence, these people called leaders are able to capture their followers's energy, loyalty, consciences, and, sometimes, even their lives. All the while, we expect our leaders to have impeccable credentials and to supply all our wants and needs.

These rare individuals rise toward the pinnacle of their ambitions with the ability to endure rejection and pain. They are equipped with an iron will to achieve their dream. They are the change masters who marched into history and have affected millions of people in days gone by. They continue to affect many people even to this day. You may love or loathe these leaders and wonder about their raison d'être, yet they overwhelm our resistance and take us where we cannot go, using their uncanny instincts to draw us into their web. They drain their followers of many things—at times including life itself—all in the name of commitment to a great and believable cause.

The world would be a dull and empty place without leaders, because they inspire us to strive toward the pinnacle of ambition to hopefully become encouragers of better things. Leaders are at times deluded, but they provide us with those sacred ingredients of inspiration and hope. When they are gone, we forget their mistakes, and they become our heroes.

Through the pages of this book, I am going to take you on a journey that may cause you to reflect on some of your perceptions and earlier understandings of the subject of leadership and, hopefully, may unsettle you enough to inspire deep, intensive thought. Whether you are already a leader or have ever dreamed of becoming one, or even if you are a faithful follower, I believe you have an honorable calling—one that cannot exist without being shackled by that strange bond of interdependency. Beware that delusions can seem real, promises are mere words, and plans often do not work out, because you are dealing with imperfect human beings and ever-changing circumstances that, fortunately or unfortunately, may also change you. Spending your life for a cause sounds noble, but it is wise to make sure that the value of the cause equals the hidden price that may be required.

Philosopher Mortimer Adler suggests that a leader must have three things: ethos, pathos, and logos. "The ethos is his moral character, the source of his ability to persuade. The pathos is the ability to touch feelings, to move people emotionally. The logos is ability to give solid reasons for an action, to move people intellectually."[2] It is not running ahead of a crowd waving a flag or grandstanding on a platform making a speech. Leadership is not a mantle to be accepted lightly. It has a price that needs to be paid intellectually, emotionally, physically, and spiritually. At times, the additional cost may be life itself.

Leadership and the power associated with it have seduced men and women since the beginning of time. While some see it as a means to help people, others choose it as the way to gain power and control for themselves. Heroes and leaders tend to rise up when confronted with a crisis, and sometimes drop back to obscurity after the job has been done. There are very few people in biblical or secular history who have occupied the pinnacle of leadership or power for any length of time without resorting to desperate and cruel means to maintain their position. The desire to obtain the submission of other human beings lurks deeply hidden beyond their personality facade.

---

2 Cyril J. Barber, *Nehemiah: An Expositional Commentary* (Eugene, OR: Wipf and Stock Publishers, 2011), 15.

We first meet them at school as the bullies or the captain of the football team. Later in life we meet them as a boss, politician, public official, successful big-business proprietor, or crook. Historians, philosophers, and behavioral scientists have been searching unsuccessfully for millennia to discover a suitable matrix or measurement that succinctly defines or creates leaders. The world's universities and institutions of higher learning still cannot answer the question, "Are leaders born or are they made?" There appears to be no teaching curriculum or set exam to obtain a degree in singular personal leadership that will qualify a person to walk automatically into a waiting leadership position with the learned ability to lead effectively.

My own leadership adventures in the past were sometimes roles I was pushed into, but on most occasions, I just stepped into a void and found myself possessed by a cause and leading it for many years. In my long and eventful life, I have been in the midst of a major national revolution, I have experienced a kidnap attempt to hold me for ransom, and at times when in dangerous situations, I have been protected by military escorts with machine guns. On one occasion, my wife and I were flying in a plane that was being shot at from the ground.

I have also had the privilege of meeting with many heads of state and famous and notable people for important dialogue. I have been both praised and vilified by the mass media. I have been interviewed and have debated on television in many countries, and I still receive international visitors from many countries who are seeking leadership counsel.

In this short book, I have included some of the knowledge that has served me well over many years. You may find it helpful if you persistently adopt it, and it may transform you into what you would like to become, but be aware that one size does not fit all!

2

THE AWAKENING PROCESS

The fact that you are reading this book indicates that you are interested in becoming a leader or are already in the process. Leadership comes in many forms and at different levels, all dependent on the individual's vision, capacity, and opportunity. Those who seek executive leadership (although vastly different in power and scope from the obligatory and heavier burden of individual leadership) will discover many of the principles and observations presented can be adjustable and adaptable.

For convenience and brevity, I am acknowledging only three levels of sole-responsibility leadership under the following categories: "short-term," relating to a cause or objective that may take several months or years to achieve; "long- term," which could be more difficult and has a larger, more impactful objective that will consume timeframes of ten years or more; and "a sense of destiny," which means the exchange of your life in the pursuit and acquisition of a measurable result. The following ten distinctives are just a small snapshot of helps, explanations, protective strategies, and principles toward the realization of the goal ahead.

Leaders do not get distracted by side issues that take more time and energy than they can afford to lose from the dominant cause. Pivotal issues must be quantified with regard to long-term effects and short-term gains, while at all times measuring the mood and perception of the followers. With any advantage gained or ground lost, the really smart leader may modify, subdue, or emphasize the action to be taken with a clever promotional spin, but to internalise fiction or half-truths as fact is the beginning of self-destruction.

Leaders are prepared to accept immediate deprivation in exchange for future gratification. Always be alert, because even a firmly laid out plan can be enhanced or sabotaged by an unexpected change of events or a new opportunity. The choice you have to make becomes an evaluation in response to several questions: First, "Will it take me off my pre-planned course?" Second, "What is the risk ratio?" Third, "How will it be received by the followers?" Fourth, "Am I being persuaded, or do I believe it would be of benefit?"

Leaders have a deep sense of reality in relation to the urgent. Self-preservation is always present in moments of crisis. Sometimes it is just a clear-cut decision to do what is right. This is where your character and willpower are challenged, and the value of your cause is forged in the fire of experience. As a general rule, successful people make decisions quickly and change them rarely, whereas unsuccessful people make decisions slowly and change them often. When a well-prepared, long-term plan has been thought out and documented, it is generally unwise to change midstream unless the basis for the plan was incomplete or there has been a major shift in the movement of events. The perception of the leader needs to be honed and matured by experience, which will develop the ability to handle bad news and put it into perspective. Only commit to the urgent when it is expedient. Do not be moved against your better judgement and never surrender your leadership. The great moral teacher Saint Augustine provided good advice when he said, "A weakened sense of responsibility does not weaken the fact of responsibility."

Leaders are prepared to accept failures with insight and optimism. Every failure has an inbuilt lesson. If you document every facet that contributed to the mistake and then reverse the procedure, it can become a building block for the future. Once accepted, the pain, the loss, and the embarrassment can be described as "weakness escaping," and this can be a great confidence-booster. Usually the first casualty in every conflict is truth, which is usually obscured by a bodyguard of lies. Truth feeds the soul, stimulates the intellect, and directs the imagination.

Leaders should not accept progress and pleasure resulting from someone else's suffering. The Chinese leader Chairman Mao Zedong once promised (but never delivered) "a chicken in every pot," and many died of malnutrition and horrific treatment under his leadership. Chairman Mao united a scattered and fragmented nation, but he disposed of his competitors with cruelty on a gigantic scale. Today the past has been put aside, and his portrait is on bank notes and posters. His name is now revered throughout the whole of China. The lesson to leaders throughout history is that you can lead by threat and terror, or lead like Mahatma Gandhi, with a promise and desire to uplift the downtrodden.

The business world is different in that it has a market monitor that is finally uncontrollable even by governments. It is simply true that your business will lead when your service or product satisfies your customers (the followers), but when the followers are taken for granted or are unable to relate to a benefit, then your leadership will quickly topple.

Leaders move from crisis to crisis, losing some and winning others, but always seeking to gain ground at every opportunity. All leaders need to have a strong sense of optimism and an irrefutable belief in their own individual ability, founded on the rock of their own conviction and moving towards a serious and credible cause. There also needs to be a recognition that in the pursuit of success, our moral conduct can at times be blinded by the challenges and passion of the struggle.

There will come a time when you are exhausted and all your energy is depleted, and then you must discover your second wind. Dr. Allen James Frances was one of the great behavioral scientists of the twentieth century. He claimed that people have a second wind, a third wind, and a fourth wind, but usually we don't push hard enough on our first wind to even discover our second wind.

Leaders need to be visible, inspirational, strong, courageous, directional, and determined. A lack of willpower is high on the list of reasons why leaders fail. Weak willpower usually hides in the shadows of conformity, and successful leaders are nonconformists. When you think outside the norm, you will stand alone until your vision becomes believable, acceptable, necessary, or doable. When you are numerically overwhelmed, ostracized, or marginalized, without support and outvoted, you must stand alone, immovable in your will and convictions, and without fear. Then you will have demonstrated your leadership.

Leaders must have the ability to inspire followers beyond the limits of what they believe to be their own capacity. There must be some stretching for all the individuals participating, while the prestige of being part of something significant means they can talk about it with pride. Guard your posture and remarks at all times and develop a commanding, enduring presence with a common touch.

Leaders must have a sense of self-denial, because you eventually become the property of "the cause." Followers may adore you or dislike you, but either way, you will realize that eventually you may even become expendable. You are not expected to get tired or be lacking in confidence at any time, and your followers will continually turn to you for answers to their many problems.

Leaders have a duty to maintain mental and physical health, which if neglected will put in jeopardy your cause and the people who are depending on you. To remain at peak performance, I made it a necessity over a forty-year period to have a country cabin with a minimum of facilities where I could go with my family to rest and be refreshed. I am sure that is the reason I have never suffered from "burnout."

HELPFUL INFORMATION

Build Exit Options Into All Plans, Procedures, and Commitments

When you are in the position of having to make a decision on the basis of information that is hearsay or has been translated through the thought processes of someone else, be very careful. You must always get the facts before responding. Some leaders, when venturing into situations they have not experienced before, factor in some kind of exit option so they can easily withdraw. You must at all times be protected by a safety valve. Do not assume!

Limiting Factors Must Always Be Tested for Reality

In a major international board meeting, we were faced with horrendous, undeserved, and untrue media coverage that was perpetrated by a disgruntled former employee. Rather than retaliate, we put the facts before the public, and the situation was overwhelmingly reported in our favor. Never rush into legal controversies or threaten anyone yourself. If you are ever involved in a legal battle that could lead to a court process, try to settle generously ... even when you are in the right. Limiting factors can be of benefit because when they are challenged and overcome, you move forward. If they can't be beaten, another way will be found, and you will grow in the process.

Priority Economics Must Be Considered in All Planning and Daily Activity (The Finance Must Be in Place)

Most leaders pass this over to an accountancy specialist and it is only brought to their attention in a crisis. My method is to ask simple questions and insist on clarity on six financial matters:

1. How much do we immediately owe?
2. How much are we committed for long term?
3. What is our cash working capital?
4. How much do we have in our reserve account?
5. What is our monthly revenue income?
6. What is our budget ratio?

There also need to be some protective measures in place, such as insurance and meeting regulatory requirements.

I was in serious discussion with the founder of a very impactful global organization who was getting older and not able to travel as much as he used to. He informed me he had just appointed a much younger and very talented president for the organization. I had known the founder for over forty years, so I felt I could ask him this important personal question. "Charlie," I said, "how do you feel passing all that power over to someone else?"

With a smile on his face and a twinkle in his eye he said, "I still control the cash!" He was still leading, but from behind.

If You Want To Keep the Bank and the Followers Happy and Be a Quality Leader, You Need To Have a Written "Transition Plan"

Let me explain. I was involved in an organization that was televised around the world, and the president was unwilling to consider having a deputy leader. Unfortunately, he collapsed while on tour overseas. Immediately the news broke. The banks shut down all accounts and asked to see the "transition plan." Unfortunately, there was no transition plan available. The organization struggled over the next few weeks as the leader recovered and things got back to normal; however, after all this, the leader refused to consider a transition plan and finally lost all his board members.

Mentors Can Be Helpful To Young Aspiring Leaders If You Understand the Process and Know How To Choose Them

The dictionary identifies a mentor as someone similar to a trusted counselor, yet in real life we would expect a great deal more than that. The summary of my involvements and observations is that the most fanciful young aspiring leaders are really seeking someone who will guide them away from mistakes, pick them up when they have failed, comfort them when they are depressed, and explain to them the secrets of success. Elijah the prophet, when confronted by Elisha with the request for his gifted abilities, (2 Kings 2:9-12), presented him with a three-point plan:

1. Keep out of the way and don't mess with what I am doing.
2. Don't be absent and expect me to be concerned. You need me; I do not need you!
3. You must watch what I do, listen to everything I say, observe the people I meet, and when the time

> comes for me to depart, you will have the ability you need.

Take special note. Elijah did not babysit Elisha! The responsibility belongs to the student.

We may seek a mentor without any consideration of who mentors the mentor or where they get their motivation from. You must seriously consider what part you expect your mentors to play in your life, whether they are responsible to be accountable, and if so, to whom. Other questions you may need to come to grips with are how to get entrance into their private world, and why they should be bothered with you anyway. Let me endeavor to provide some answers that may be of some help.

My first mentor had poise, presence, and confidence that put people at ease. In contrast, I was awkward, self-conscious, and hesitant. I wanted what he had, and if I could get his attention and interest in my life, I was convinced I would learn. After making some inquiries, I discovered that he was buying a new automobile and was considering building a spacious brick garage. I am a first-class bricklayer and informed him that if he supplied the material, I would build the walls free of charge. Needless to say, he accepted. I spent every Saturday working at his private home until the garage was completed, and we became firm friends. I learned to give first, and the benefit to me was life changing.

My next mentor was an expert in marketing, which was foreign to me. He had just moved into a new home that needed cement paving, and at that time, skilled tradesmen were very hard to find. I offered to do a special type of decorative paving for him. I spent time with him and his family and learned the dynamics of marketing.

My subsequent mentor was a much older man who was an economic business genius, and he needed my youthful enthusiasm and energy. Through this arrangement, I received the understanding I needed.

As the years progressed, my life changed and I became deeply involved relating on equal terms with my long-term heroes. I never forgot my lessons, and in my later years I was able to help others. The mentor has no responsibility toward the aspirant, so the question must be asked and answered: What is the benefit for the mentor? Quite a bit, really. The mentor in turn acquires a younger, energetic, hungry-to-learn person who is eager to assist him or her at no cost and could become a life-time friend and supporter.

MY MENTORING PRINCIPLES

- If you have no one to relate to, then search for past historical heroes and study their lives together with the economic and social climate in which they lived. If you want to be a leader, the quickest way is to use a number of mentors, each with different capabilities and availability.
- Do not treat your mentors with too much familiarity. I always used the title Mr. or Mrs., or their professional title, with great respect.
- Choose mentors for their achievement level, not because they flatter you.
- Over time, as change takes place and your boundaries expand, you may need to change your mentors.
- Beware of greedy mentors who will use your willingness and make extravagant promises and teach you nothing but humiliating servitude.

- In the final analysis, why don't you find someone who is less experienced than you who needs a mentor, and help them?

There will come a time as an aspiring leader that you will need to be ready to collide with a great opportunity. This was succinctly summed up in the words of Abraham Lincoln: "I will study, I will prepare, and my opportunity will come." Opportunities do not come with a value stamped on them, and intelligence and learning do not mean you are ready to grasp a great opportunity. You must strive to develop the qualities of perception, reason, judgement, and inspiration that are needed to turn opportunities into actions.

There is a principle much overlooked in effective and progressive leadership, which is that the authority and power to exact penalties automatically invokes respect and, at times, some fear. Without the power to impose a penalty, the mantle of leadership remains sterile and is reduced to weak, subjective management. The inflicting of a penalty can only be carried out if the rules are clear, and it must be prompt and fair. Joshua was probably one of the best-trained leaders in history, and when God laid the mantle of leadership on him, He said that the nations would fear him (Deuteronomy 2:25).

> **IT IS IMPERATIVE FOR YOU TO GAIN RESPECT EARLY, AND FOR THAT TO BECOME A REALITY, YOU MUST MOVE FROM INTENTIONS TO RESULTS WHILE AT THE SAME TIME ENSURING THAT YOUR IDEOLOGY AND STRATEGY ARE NEVER IN CONFLICT.**

It is imperative for you to gain respect early, and for that to become a reality, you must move from intentions to results, while at the same time ensuring that your ideology and strategy are never in conflict. The other two leadership styles are consensus and terror, and neither have a heroic history of great events. The germ of great ideas or a plan usually has its birth in the mind of the individual. A group may finally confirm what needs to be done, but they rarely initiate the thought.

Leaders have strong opinions based on tested beliefs and deep, strong convictions. They will not bow to threats, pressure, or numbers. In some circumstances, they will deliberately move against the crowd on issues of timing or structure, because they understand the lurking dangers and see the full picture. This can cause anger in the ranks, but all leaders are mindful of the fact that moods can be changed, and they are masters of persuasion.

Leaders are there for one reason, and that is to get the job done! They are there to obtain your loyalty and energy. They are not there for affection. It is quite natural for leaders to be lonely in the midst of a crowd as they study body language and listen for nuances to assess the mood of the people they are leading.

In 1933, when Adolf Hitler was rising in power, he was asked how he would handle the huge masses of people that were following him. His prompt response was simple but profound. He said, "Don't be so concerned with the followers; all they require is bread and circuses to make them happy." Hitler understood clearly that in difficult times, the followers yearn for someone who will offer security with a promise of a better lifestyle.

Leaders have a different mindset from followers because they obtain their stimulation not by security, but from risk and delayed gratification. They have an inbuilt understanding that as events unfold, new opportunities will emerge. When in discussions on leadership, be alert to misconceptions and faulty logic when someone offers military quotes and clichés to remedy a civil leadership situation. It may provide some comic relief and sound interesting, but it rarely fits.

Never laugh at your mistakes, but treat your errors of speech or action as a serious opportunity to correct and learn. When you make a mistake or error of judgement, do not dwell on how much it hurt you, but rather focus on what it taught you.

Many years ago, as a much younger man, I was part of a large live-in weekend convention, and I had a minor responsibility in the management of the youth program. At the conclusion of all the meetings, the senior lecturers invited me to join them to take part in a comical race over a short distance with a pumped-up balloon held between our knees and a porcelain plate with an egg on it held in our hands to see who would win the race without dropping the egg. I refused to participate, because I understood that sometime in the future I would be a leader, and I did not want any ridiculous photographs around that could be used to trivialize my effectiveness.

In later years, when I was much older and chairman of the board of directors of a large organization, we took our senior management to an island resort for some intense upgrading training, and there were to be some festivities on the closing evening. My board members were all preparing to wear fancy costumes at the party and wanted me to have the superman outfit, but I respectfully declined. I also insisted that all directors and managers remain suitably dressed. I explained to them that they shouldn't risk having their funny photographs pinned on the noticeboard in the lunch room, because it could minimize the respect and authority that they had worked so hard to obtain.

If you are aspiring to leadership, always be alert to the fact that in the future, your past, as well as your present, may become public news. Be very careful of posed photographs of any kind, and be particularly mindful of who is standing on each side of you. I was once photographed with my wife on one side and a young female model on the other, and guess what? When the magazine was published, my wife was cut out and the young model and I stood together on a feature page.

In leadership, you have to remain motivated at all times. Although motivation can be contagious, it must come from the top down, not from the bottom up. Such motivation always comes with a sense of the future, and it becomes a magnet that draws people toward you.

Discourage intrusion into your preferred areas; otherwise, responsibilities will overlap, and energies and efficiency will be reduced. Under intense pressure, and even when alone, reason will sometimes take a back seat. At that moment, you need to activate thought displacement and stand sentinel at the gate of your mind and challenge your own thought patterns. You must not let your creative subconscious mind take you along a path that leads you where do not want to go.

As a leader, you need to be courteous to everyone, but select your close friends with care. My criteria for friendship have served me well for over fifty years and may be of help to you:

- Friends must be honest—I do not want to have to put a percentage point on the accuracy of everything they tell me.
- They need a sense of humor—We need to be able to laugh at ourselves occasionally.
- I want my friends to be big thinkers and have empires in their brains.
- They must be generous with their money, time, and abilities.

One of the attributes of a good leader is the skill of communication. It has many facets. The sound of your voice, the flow of words, and your body language are interrelated and can endorse or destroy the message you want to transmit. There needs to be sensitivity to people of varying intelligence. Deep thought, intensive preparation, and practice are required to be able, by voice and words alone, to move people from their comfort zone into prompt and long-term action.

Winston Churchill is a wonderful example. By voice and tone, he turned a timid, unprepared nation into a fighting force as he skillfully and passionately sent the English language into battle. Churchill's call to arms was not an off-the-cuff speech; it was carefully crafted and repeatedly practised to enable it to flow. He turned it into a lightning rod that convicted and inspired all who heard it, stimulating them to rise above the average and commit beyond the thrill of courage. Churchill understood that people are complicated animals and become simpler under pressure.

Communication has many facets, including the written word, the delivery of an oral instruction first-hand or by a telephone call or a speech, or by a third person. Even if they are all identical in clarity and substance, each one can be prone to error or misinterpretation in the hearing. When you are checking for clarity, ask the person receiving the message what they thought the message meant, not what you said. You may get a surprising answer!

When you are preparing to make a speech and you want to be understood, you have to make sure you have made yourself intelligible. When you have to address a crowd, make sure you prepare well in advance. Practise your speech to remove repetition and avoid reciting it in a jerky or flat monotone. This is your big chance to get your vision across and inspire your followers, who could be similarly inspiring when they repeat what you've said to others.

Here is a simple formula I have used for fifty years and which has never failed me:

- Develop a dynamic theme.
- Create a good story line.
- Use some drama in your presentation.
- Keep to short, easily understood phrases.
- Modulate your voice for emphasis.
- Inspire loyalty to your cause.

Napoleon was a master at gaining loyalty from his troops. (This is one of the rare military situations you could modify for civil use.) Napoleon would put aside time in the evening before the next morning's battle and ask his officers to name and describe the features of twenty of the soldiers who would be on parade for inspection before the attack. He would want to know the names and members of their families. He would stay up late into the night memorizing all the details. The next morning at dawn, he would walk up and down the ranks, calling those soldiers by name and inquiring about members of their family. Then he would utter the words, "Fight well, my sons." The message, "He cares for us all," would sweep through the ranks, and they would go out and fight to the death for him. Many famous leaders in history—and even today—are appreciated and revered by their followers because of their speeches and their commanding presence, coupled with a genuine common touch.

Communication is not unloading on your audience! That is why you must be careful. Avoid placing yourself before people when you are sick, tired, angry, or fearful, because under those abnormal conditions, your intuitive alertness could be impaired, and this could create a disturbing uneasiness about your leadership stability.

3

TIME—THE IMMOVABLE DIMENSION

You can die with more money than you can spend, and with many dreams unfulfilled, and when you die, there is no more time available to you. Time is the very essence of life itself and is irrecoverable. We are living in a time of speedy communication that also expects speedy completion of projects; however, being in a world of information overload at times increases the workload and reduces our time off. Finding a way to shrink the amount of time needed to get things done is no sooner achieved than we have to face a new and better way to do the same things! Obsolescence has become a way of life, yet we continue to make better gadgets and machinery that lasts longer. Even human beings are experiencing longevity, but we do not know what to do with them when we keep extending their use-by date.

Many of our young people learn things at university they may never use when they graduate. Instead, they may work for the failed students who become the entrepreneurs and provide them with jobs. We spend more and more time on our smartphones and do not use the very thing that was given to us at birth and resides between our ears; it remains undisturbed and of little use.

There are those in our communities who live in constant fear of losing their jobs because of the continuing pressure to get more and more done, when there is rarely enough time to get the job completed on time, let alone have any time left over for extra tasks. We smugly accept as normal financial budget overruns and extensions of time beyond what has been agreed to in signed contracts, and then call out to the government to take up the shortfall to maintain employment. It is almost accepted practice for governments to support inefficiency and go on correcting the errors of avoidable problems.

Now in the twenty-first century, we must ask the question, "Are we expecting too much from the human machine?" Is it possible that the cumbersomeness and confusion that besets our lives, future programs, and work schedules can be overcome effectively by creating space? This would result not only in relief for leaders and participants, but it would also improve their quality of life.

Husbands, wives, children, families, and friends continually complain that there is not enough time available to savor those sweet moments when they can be together or just enjoy being alone. I believe and have proven in my long life of activity that there are six lifestyle principles that can assist us to accomplish this. I call these "My Lifetime Code of Conduct."

MY LIFETIME CODE OF CONDUCT

A Simple Lifestyle

The most common cause of overwork and the lack of time is confusion about where you are now in your life in relation to where you want to be and how you plan to get there. The appearance of activity that can sometimes elicit admiration and naively be perceived as a strong achievement program may be doing little more than burning up energy, wasting time, and creating more stress.

Most problems in time management begin with a lifestyle created by a lack of thought, by the imitation of others, or by accepting the incorrect notion that you are made the way you are and cannot change. Psychologists have told me that I am an introvert, although it is not apparent to those who see me in action or those who are involved with me in business. From my perspective, it is a matter of choice. I prefer the atmosphere of solitude on a horse or a camel in the outback of Australia to the buzz of large crowds or television studios.

It is possible that you can even develop a lifestyle contrary to your perceived personality style and outside of your comfort zone. The first step is to understand and come to grips with what your comfort zone is, and then use it as a benchmark to measure your progress towards those areas of discipline that make for a successful and fulfilling life. There will be times that you will be drawn back to your comfort zone, but knowing where it is will remove the vagueness that may lead to vacillation. You may need to confront yourself with a "fear list" and reason it through to gain some new insights into your present personality and to clarify your value system.

The next step is to accept some practical changes that will release you to get more done and still have time left over. Try to adopt an uncluttered lifestyle. Get rid of incidentals and encumbrances that limit your effectiveness and will only burn up time and energy.

I would continually check to make sure people and events were keeping to schedule with a motto, "Don't expect if you don't inspect." Giving someone a job to do and expecting it to be done to a standard and on time is a fallacy if you don't continually inspect.

Concentrate On the Essentials

There have been times when I have had to travel constantly for six weeks, and I have been met at airports and greeted with surprise because I only had one luggage bag and a carry-on, and no assistant. The reason is simple:

- I only have one pair of shoes and a dark suit with spare trousers, three shirts and ties, and, of course, underwear and toiletries.
- I carry my office and communication needs in a wheel-on briefcase.
- I have never had a personal assistant, because I know what is going on better than anyone else and can say "yes" or "no" faster than anyone else. Of course, I have a secretary back at the office on twenty-four-hour call. (My wife thinks it strange that when I need a new pair shoes, I leave the old shoes in the shop and walk out wearing the new ones. Anything I have not worn for six months I obviously don't need, so I simply give away.) In this new day and age of personal computers, I answer emails on the run.

In an earlier era—the 1970s and towards the year 2000—we had the exciting experience of the meteoric capitalist rise of Japan and Europe, booms, recessions, and the oil crisis. Now we have before us the ever-expanding giant of China that is all but dominating world attention. No longer can we predict the ebb and flow of goods and services, and we may never return to a comparatively stable global climate of power and economics with the security of any predictability.

If you have concerns for your future as a leader of a cause or a business organization, why not create your own fear list and imagine the worst possible case scenario that could take place? I call this my "Achilles' heel," or my most vulnerable position. Having made my fear list, I immediately conduct a commando raid on all activities and liabilities, searching for the hidden enemy.

Let me present you with a real-life situation that should resonate with everyone reading this book. I was on the board of directors of the largest and most successful replacement aluminium window manufacturer in the southern hemisphere. They were leaders in their field during a time of fierce competition for sales. We met for a board meeting to discuss a strategy to fight the strong challenges facing our position in the market place.

The general consensus of the board was that we were strong, and several of the board members were sitting back comfortably while smoking their cigars with pleasure. One of the prominent men suggested an expansion plan with satellite plants around the larger cities of Australia, and another went even further, recommending extending overseas, to which suggestion there were considered responses.

Unbeknown to the chairman and other board members, the week before I had spent half a day walking around the large plant, talking to workers and managers and asking questions and taking notes. I finished up in the lunch room with the employees, enjoyed their jokes, and then followed them back to their tasks.

With my mind still reeling from my in-depth visit a week earlier, and having observed the waste, inefficiency, and casualness of the plant managers that extended down to the scattered disposal of rubbish and the inefficient office procedures, I was ready to explode! I asked the chairman if I could address both him and the board. He readily agreed with the acclamation of all present.

As I stood, I faced the chairman (who had started the business from his home). He smiled at me pleasantly and with a hand gesture said, "The floor is yours." Knowing him on friendly terms, I addressed myself directly to him and said, "Robin, many years ago, as a younger man hungry to succeed, you conceived an idea to build aluminum window frames to replace the many wooden ones that were falling apart in old homes. It was and still is a brilliant idea. Your only tools were a hacksaw, a grinding and cutting machine, some measuring instruments, a few hand tools, and a guillotine, much of it burdened with borrowed money. Is that basically correct?"

He smilingly nodded and replied, "With a lot of borrowed money."

I continued, "Robin, I want you to think now as that younger man with the hunger and energy you had to succeed back then. My question to you is this: Could you beat this large organization in price, quality, and service?"

The room remained silent for a few minutes as he looked at the ceiling, and then breathing out the smoke from his cigar, he said slowly, emotionally, and firmly, "I would easily bury that company."

My quick response to Robin and the rest of the directors was to tell them of my earlier visit to the plant and provide details from my notes of some of the glaring problems that required attention. I went on to say, "We are in trouble because we have become fat, complicated, sloppy, and overloaded with staff, equipment, and rules. We need to devise a crisis plan immediately!"

While the rest of the directors did not agree that my analysis revealed they were following a recipe for a crisis, they did take some limited steps that I believed were insufficient. However, I felt my usefulness on that board had expired, so I resigned. They continued to lose ground over the next few years, and today they are out of business.

Now is the time to ask yourself the question: "If war, financial collapse, fire, illness, bereavement, embezzlement, or market change in your industry came, how would you retain and improve your lifestyle?" Create a simple lifestyle and stay ahead of the game.

Control Your Time

I can almost hear you saying, "It is just not possible ... you don't understand! Because I am a leader, how can I deny myself to others? It seems I am expected to be available twenty-four hours a day!"

Have you ever considered what your life is worth? It is a time allocation that is exclusively yours, so control it! Let's use some elementary logic and pose some questions you have probably never considered. How much longer do you expect to have an effective working life and still maintain your physical well-being? What is the full value of your intellect and your spiritual capacity? Think, and think hard! If you had to put a monetary value on your life from this moment until you die and be a permanent slave to someone else, what price would you put on it? Think of the hidden genius that is still within you that has not yet been released. What price would you put on your experience, dreams, aspirations, and heritage? Confronting, isn't it? And the only person who can fully determine that figure is you! Once you begin to define your value, you are already accepting that it is also exclusively yours to be wasted, given away, sold on the auction block of employment, or used for growth and enjoyment.

I have at times walked a mile to the state public library, and there, in a quiet solitary atmosphere beyond the reach of telephones and isolated from all personal, business, and other cares, I have guaranteed for myself a timeslot that is exclusive and interruption-proof. Why don't you find a quiet spot in your area, away from distractions and interruptions, and set aside a timeslot to do your most demanding and important tasks? You will find that a concentrated time of freedom to work without any impediment to your work flow will multiply what you get done and will provide some time left over as well!

Continually evaluate your position each morning or at the beginning of the week. Then set out what must be done and put necessary time aside to complete each item. Arrange everything else around these requirements and learn to say "no" to those irritating items and requests that seem to squeeze out the things that must be done. Be vigilant—no compromise! Make it a contest of your will against the circumstances that continually beset you. Press on until finally it becomes a natural habit ... and believe for success.

Make your telephone subject to your convenience. If you don't, it can be the most demanding of all masters, caring neither for good manners, fairness, or decorum, but relentlessly and persistently interrupting and creating havoc in your schedule.

I have a very influential overseas friend who would overlook international time zones and call me on my private number at home, often at 2:00 a.m. Unfortunately, he had a loud, penetrating voice, and when he said, "Peter, buddy," I almost hit the ceiling with fright. Of course, he would apologise for mistaking the time, but it would be impossible for me to go back to sleep. This went on and on for months. Eventually, I deliberately phoned him several times at 2:00 a.m. in his time zone, and his calls were suddenly and permanently adjusted.

My son, Graham, carries two phones—one that is 24/7 for family, and one for the rest of the world that he turns off completely for respite one day a week. Interruptions must be discouraged if we are serious about the programs we have committed ourselves to complete.

To stay informed and expand your thinking capacity, you will need to have a reading method of accuracy and speed to provide you with the information you are seeking. It becomes easier if you know what your mission in life is and focus on the following:

- Information:
  By absorbing information that does not relate to your mission in life, you become a wasteful information gatherer. Stay focused and only document that which is useful and adaptable.
- Principles:
  These are the characteristic building blocks towards specific desired achievements. Just as music, engineering, medicine, and beliefs have a set of principles to undergird their practical application, so life formulae and rules act as signals that provide security and confidence.
- Key phrases:
  All human beings are responsive to words and the tone in which they are presented. Words inform, explain, enthuse, and motivate. When reading, I sometimes find electrifying, short compositions of words that convey a personality or situation with such clarity and feeling that it immediately arrests my response bank and is stored for later use.

Apply Strong Pressure to Specific Tasks

Look for items on your agenda that can be accelerated, and be courageous to avoid becoming a coward through conformity. Most people prefer to be static, because it feels secure.

Life is full of waiting time, obsolete functions, errors, and margins, but time improvements can be found in the most unlikely places, and the search will exist as long as mankind continues to compete. We wonder if we are on the right track, maintaining sufficient pace, applying the best method, or utilising our best skills ... and the list continues.

On one occasion, in a moment of deep thought, I came up with a solution that eradicated two functions that had no effect on the end results and freed up precious time. At another time, I was waiting for my luggage at an airport when we were advised over the loudspeaker that the conveyer belt had jammed, and I would have to wait four hours for my luggage to be released. I had an important meeting commencing in two hours and it seemed an impossible situation. As I watched the luggage porter roll his eyes in disbelief, I went to him and gave him a twenty-dollar bill and asked him if he would climb up the chute and retrieve my bag. I had it back within five minutes. Sometimes money can save you time and prove relatively inexpensive. Don't be timid about offering cash.

Carriers and suppliers need to be reminded that continuing to do business with us depends upon our satisfaction. A friend of mine tells me that he changes gas stations and banks every two years because by that time they take you for granted, and the level of service drops. Those who are involved with you need to be reminded on occasion of the level of commitment and skill required to ensure your satisfaction with them, and know that the continuity of their position with you depends on this.

Try this to get things moving. Get to work very early for one or two weeks and set tight timeframes for specific work to be completed, with penalties for failure and rewards for results, allowing free time for a job well done. Treat yourself the same way, and the results will surprise you! Take heed and do not be a permanent pressure-cooker to yourself or others around you, otherwise you may burst the pipes and have people walk out on you. Always create a friendly, competitive atmosphere, looking towards the end results and the rewards available. Turn problems into procedures.

How often have you heard someone say that they are always making the same mistakes and then laugh it off and continue on?

One of the greatest time-wasters is repetitive error, and unfortunately it becomes habit-forming. Build some character traits in your team that encourage people to do things right the first time. This will prevent you from being robbed of time by avoidable repetition.

The biblical book of Ecclesiastes talks about "a time for every purpose under heaven, (Ecclesiastes 3:1-8)," and the great writer Charles Dickens, in the opening chapter of his book *A Tale of Two Cities*, states, "It was the best of times and it was the worst of times." It seems that every generation wrestles with the elusive mystery of time, and every creature and plant on earth has an inbuilt timeframe that governs its growth and, ultimately, its direction and expiration. Only human beings have the unlimited creative capacity and the opportunity to make time work for them and pass helpful information on to the next generation.

The challenge to all of us is to be creative by conserving and expanding our time, because, unlike money and other gifts we have in life, time is unredeemable and therefore limited.

Choose Words Carefully and Accurately to Save Time

A great deal of unnecessary work is caused by the need to resolve misunderstandings and to clarify instructions and comments.

Poor communication can lead to arguments, suspicion, and polarization of groups, all of which wastes time. To get more done and have time left over means you must aim at clarity in what you say and, very often, in the tone you use. In English, the meaning of many words can be completely changed by tone of voice alone, and if written phonetically, a great deal of our language can become quite confusing. For specific results, use specific tools:

- Exactly what do I want to achieve by my statement?

- How do I expect the recipient to respond?
- Clarify, in writing if necessary, exactly what you want to say.
- Practise using the correct tone of voice for what you want to convey.

All too often a communication problem is created because we shovel words out of our mouths with the same abandonment we use to shovel snow, and then later we have to backtrack and reinterpret what was said, knowing that what was originally said has in some way misdirected the outcome.

When you have to correct a situation, make it perfectly clear that you understand the mistake and what must be done to correct it. Many years ago, I was the sales director of a company when the chairman of the board, with the termination salary in hand, went to dismiss a young lady who was not doing her job properly. He told the young lady he thought it would be best that she leave. In response, the girl said she did not agree and thought there was room for negotiation. He then walked into my office still holding the envelope with her severance pay in it, shaking his head with a confused look on his face. I immediately took the envelope out of his hand and went and told her she was fired. Within ninety seconds, I was back in my office, with the chairman of the board standing there, stunned by what had happened.

Confront others and situations promptly, and let people know your standards, without malice or hardness, but with clarity and warmth. Do not repeat yourself! Get into the habit of saying things once, without causing any misunderstanding. Repeat instructions rarely, if at all, and you will always command attention and usually get action. Your communication time will be halved, and your productivity will skyrocket. Your time left over will reflect the difference!

When confronting others, use "the role and identity method," separating the person from the role. I would speak to the person along these lines: "Jim, you are a very likeable person and you have many talents in areas where I do not. As a person, you are quite unique. But Jim, there is another side that does not reflect upon your person, but rather your role in this organization, and that is quite distinct from who you are. Your role in this organization is to manage our books, and in that area, your work has not measured up to the standards we have set."

The difference is that you are not attacking the person, but centering on the role, which, of course, is the real problem. By all means available to you, help those who need help. But to permanently help and support people means that you, not they, are living out their lives. All tasks have standards, and everyone needs to find the standard that is best suited to them to make them happy and useful. For you to support someone on a permanent basis because they are unable to cope in a situation tends to demean the person's dignity and relegate them to a position of less than what could be.

There are, of course, those who unfortunately have some genuine disability. They need and should have the best help available, and I would help them get it.

Always try to employ and associate with those who are reliable. Life is usually made up of choices, not chances, and we inevitably get out of life that which we choose, or that which comes to us because we did not make a choice. In leadership, business, or pleasure you have some choices in respect to those with whom you become involved. For example, you can get a transfer, change jobs or professions, move to another location, or choose a different climate. The world is a big place of choices, particularly where democracy prevails, and usually choice becomes a matter of personal preferences. Your time is a limited investment that needs to be protected, so determine the limits of tolerable behavior.

> **LIFE IS USUALLY MADE UP OF CHOICES, NOT CHANCES, AND WE INEVITABLY GET OUT OF LIFE THAT WHICH WE CHOOSE OR THAT WHICH COMES TO US BECAUSE WE DID NOT MAKE A CHOICE.**

While it may seem unusual to write about these issues in relation to time management, it only takes a little reflection to realize just how much time is wasted by associating with those who are not reliable. You are not responsible for their behavior if you have been fair in your dealings with them. If they have chosen to ignore your tolerance, you should move on and get more done and have time left over. So,

- give clear, specific directions;
- confront problems promptly;
- think, then speak;
- say it once; and
- look for reliable associates.

Time Alone and Time at Work Are of Equal Value

My most important work gets done when I am alone. As I reflect, imagine, and plan, my thought processes become stimulated and productive. If you are a woodcutter, you need to stop to sharpen your axe; if you are a pastor of a church, you need to revitalize your spirit; if you are an athlete, you need to relax and rest your body; if you are a soldier, rest and recreation times are imperative for you to maintain your balance and resilience.

The leader and the entrepreneur may need more quality solitude than employees or those who are in more predictable positions, because leaders need stimuli, and in large proportions. For many years, my wife has asked me to take more time off for holidays and rest, not realizing that most of my revitalization comes from the diverse situations in which I often find myself. However, I did make a commitment to her that if a time were to come when the cut and thrust of my many involvements did not provide for me what I felt was required to get the best out of myself, I would take a long period of rest and reflection—and in time, I did.

Over the years I would stay in a private study room in the state library just to think and plan. I always found that each time I did that, the future became more exciting and the jumps in capacity were quantum. The biblical quotation, *"The generous soul will be made rich, And he who waters will also be watered himself"* (Proverbs 11:25, NKJV), is true. This is why we must not only be involved with others, but also governed by a predetermined goals program.

Treat all commitments as moral obligations and do not commit yourself to what you cannot or do not want to do. Put a measurement of time and value on everything. Money is simply minted personality. If you have enough time, you can always earn more money, but money cannot buy you one more moment of time. The following are some reminders to allow you to get more done and have plenty of time left over:

- Check that appointments are still at the agreed time and location.
- Send emails of clarification after negotiations.
- Do not overlook that which you do not understand.
- Build in financial and time reserves for all occasions.
- Remember the bluntest pencil is sharper than best memory. Write things down.
- Get interruption-free time to do important tasks.
- Simplify everything.

- Do things in order of importance, not in order of irritation or pressure.
- Always have cash reserves.
- Do not commit yourself in haste.
- Put a percentage measurement on all your time commitments.
- Speak clearly and precisely.
- Confront carefully and always leave the door open.
- Do not do for yourself what others can do better and more cheaply.
- Control the telephone for your benefit.
- Make a list of your business essentials and forget the gimmicks and gadgets.
- Plan long term and keep to your plan.

TIME FOR WHAT?

The time left over will create a measurement of your life's value, because it will reflect your assessment of the great gift called life. You can squander time left over with self-indulgence that will not stand the test of time and benefit no one, including yourself, or you can go for permanence and spend time helping others who are less fortunate than you are, creating the love and gratitude that transcends time. You can spend time with those you love, enhancing and complimenting them with the most precious of all the gifts you have to give— your personal time

4

DON'T KNOW WHAT'S WRONG? TRY THIS.

You may have a good board of directors or group of advisors. They may seem to be bright, intelligent human beings with some special expertise that you need. But you are frustrated, because you are finding it difficult to get consensus on important issues, and you are just about ready to get rid of them all and try some fresh blood. You have a gut feeling that something is going on that you just can't put your finger on, and it's driving you crazy. The answer could be that you have a power manipulator in your midst.

Let me explain. My good friend, John, is one of the smartest men I know. He was president of one of the world's largest confectionery manufacturing companies. He was so capable and successful that he was given almost total power, and he had enormous influence at many levels of business and society.

When we were having breakfast together one morning, he shared with me that he was having some frustrations with his board of directors, who created strange delays and obstructions. On top of this, vital information was leaking out. When he challenged the board of directors and his management team, they all seemed to come up clean. He had to be away for a few days interstate, and he asked me to have a private lunch with his board members to see if I could discover anything.

When John arrived back a few days later, he was anxious to know if I had anything to report to him that could throw some light on the situation. My response took him by surprise. I told him that he had a sneaky power manipulator and a stooge on his board who were causing all the trouble, and that they should both be promptly fired! I went on to explain the profile of power manipulators and how easy it is to identify them. It is a well-known and indisputably accepted fact that all leaders are actual or potential power holders, but not all power holders are leaders.

Power manipulators are people who feel safer and protected in the role of ultimate adviser with no liability. Because of their personality, they find it almost impossible to cope with accepting full personal responsibility. Consequently, they find their fulfilment by becoming power manipulators, and in this way, they gain satisfaction and prestige without personal commitment.

Power manipulators are those who arrive late at meetings, and by that delay exercise their power to restrain and cause all the proceedings to be repeated to an audience of one. The power manipulator then occupies center stage and questions the whole team on trivial issues relating to earlier discussions. Power manipulators easily identify themselves in meetings when decisions or commitments are about to be made by saying, "I am not sure about that," or some similar phrase, to gain a pivotal point of control. The obvious thing to do is to suggest an alternative or withhold comment. Power manipulators ask long and detailed questions, but do nothing constructive or positive with the answers, and they finally become wasteful information gatherers.

By this time John was starting to smile, but I continued and explained that power manipulators seek specific clarification on obscure issues, which if acted upon, produce very little and add nothing of substance to the meeting. Power manipulators seek more and more information when they are not using the information they already have. They take no direct measurable responsibility and tend to direct issues through other people to avoid personal commitment. By stealth, they obligate other people to respond directly to them. These power holders guard their power posture by refraining from being in any position where they are compelled to respond to others. In meetings and discussions, they use silence or non-verbal facial expressions that create questions, doubt, and mystique. By skillfully using silence as a tool, they can neither be condemned nor praised until that silence is broken by voice, posture, written word, or action.

Classic power manipulators may even befriend you to gain some intimate information that allows them to have influence over your thoughts and direction, and then use it against you later for their own protection or benefit. Power manipulators defend or provoke an action or thought based on a principle without any real personal commitment to that principle as long as they are not implicated or adversely affected. These power manipulators are not restricted to the boardroom; they are present in all areas of life and easily identified.

When I finished, John slapped his hand on the table and said, "You have described them to me perfectly, and I know who they are!" He promptly fired them both. Problem solved!

If that is not where the problem is, then you need to look further and investigate the following seven trigger points to find the trouble spot:

1. Follow the money. Someone may be expanding expenses or getting kickbacks and covering up for goods not received. This is called "funny money."
2. There may be some favoritism or romance at the executive level and a possible sexual cover-up.

3. Someone may be withholding information to protect their control position or in order to prolong their employment.
4. There may be envy and jealousy within the ranks because someone feels let down or unfairly marginalized.
5. Someone may be hiding the facts for fear of the consequences.
6. Someone may lack the competence to carry out the required job and be hiding behind delays and excuses.
7. There may be "foot-dragging," which is mental or physical laziness.

Almost every blockage, obstacle, obstruction, or refusal to perform or follow through on a direction given by a leader can usually be traced to one of these seven cover-up techniques. The very essence of all leadership lies in your ability to get your followers to participate in the necessary corrections. The leader who has the ability to do that has a powerful leverage on the world.

Skilled leadership and the wise use of the power that is associated with it may require a re-shuffling of personnel when long-held positions become comfort zones and begin to stagnate the growth of the organization. Good leadership must continually seek opportunities that will have the greatest positive effect on the success of the overall program and result in the least possibility of damage to the overall cause.

> **EVERY LEADER WILL BE CONFRONTED WITH A CRISIS.**

The great Albert Einstein said (and he was right), "Imagination is more important than knowledge." In your leadership, you need to imagine how the future is going to be and prepare and plan for it, allowing for variables. There is always a wide gap between what ought to be done and what finally gets done, and a leader must continually generate the power required by the use of spiritual, emotional, and intelligent energy.

Every leader will be confronted with a crisis. Interestingly, the word crisis has a special double meaning in the Asiatic world. It is understood to mean "danger and opportunity." I will share one of my many experiences in a major crisis situation that took place many years ago. I walked into my private elevator and pressed the button to the top floor. I stepped into the foyer of our penthouse, all the time trying to understand and recover from a heavy day filled with almost insurmountable problems. Interest rates from banks for investment in real estate development were becoming shaky. I had my own and clients' money invested in three countries, and the ability to maintain a strong cash flow and profit could soon become unsustainable.

All business confidence took a nosedive. Some desperate operators were expecting only a short recession and were illegally using their trust money to bridge the gap, and unfortunately some months later went to prison. I tried to get my head around it and finally gave up and went to bed, only to wake up in the middle of the night. In my pajamas, I went down the elevator to my international headquarters and began to think thoughts that to my surprise began to inspire me. I felt prompted to write these words on my desk blotting paper: "When our strong optimistic desire to think, commit, and work exceeds by far our weak, negative fear of failure, then success is always guaranteed!" Suddenly optimism took the front seat, and I immediately started to create a plan to plug up the economic gaps, cut costs, and stimulate profit from wherever it was to be found.

I thought I had it beaten, but two weeks later the words I wrote on the blotting paper in the middle of the night did not seem relevant anymore, and everything began to accelerate and close in on me. I was now faced with a gigantic economic crisis that was about to wipe me out. In total confusion, I decided to go for a swim in our pool, and as I was lying on my back in the water looking up at sky in deep thought, I was unaware that my wife, Robina, was watching and sensing my anguish.

She said, "I am your wife, and I need to know what is bothering you."

My response was very dismissive. I said, "You can't handle it."

Robina said, "Then do what you believe needs to be done, and I am with you all the way." (What an incredible support!)

Immediately, I took control of my attitude, accepted full responsibility, and documented the facts.

I had faced many difficulties before and understood that problems always appear to expand under pressure, so I needed to confront the situation and clearly put it into perspective. I knew that events would move swiftly and that I needed to be first to discount and sell, so I cut the price of much of my stock by 40 percent and got it quickly sold while others traders were holding out for higher prices. Many of their businesses collapsed and they went to the wall, some never to recover.

I left my son, Graham, to deal with our remaining creditors and set about finding new ways to make money again. Within two years, the pressure was off. The major crisis turned out to be a great benefit, and later we ended up financially stronger than ever before.

The method I used to handle this crisis involved steps that proved to be useful and can be applied to resolve any crisis successfully:

1. List on a large sheet all the problems you have, including the collateral fallout expected.
2. Allocate percentage points to each, estimating the anticipated loss of money, people, direction, and influence.
3. On a score of 1 to 10, rate the danger and magnitude of each, measured in quantity and time.
4. Check your list again and again, and do not kid yourself.
5. When it is all completed, pin it on the back of your office or bedroom door and make sure to update it, positively or negatively, as changing circumstances direct.
6. Get all minor nuisance problems out of the way and meet individually with those oppressing you with the intention of slowing you down or minimizing your problem.

I was careful not to make commitments that I could not keep, and on that basis, I would re-adjust what I had previously written on my planning sheet.

When you are facing a major problem and are working on a plan to survive, your mind will be razor sharp, and you should consider working on a plan of recovery for when the crisis is over. Don't wait to do it when you are relaxed, as then your brain will have slowed down and your desperation quotient will be lower.

5

PLANS TO ACHIEVE

Your present declares your courage.
Your past established your character.
Your future demonstrates your vision.
Your final exit is your heritage.

As a young man, I was intrigued by the achievements of the great leaders of history, and I marveled at their superior willpower and directional dedication. This sent me on a permanent journey studying history and biographies, which still enthral me to this day. I used to spend days at the great library in the city searching for answers to two questions:

1. Is there a tried and tested method, formula, or matrix for goal setting?
2. Is there a tried and tested method, formula, or matrix for creating a mission statement?

I could find nothing, and it became my sacred quest to find the answers! I was fortunate in my business and philanthropic pursuits to have interactive dialogue with many successful and famous people. I took opportunities with individuals of great age who could recall first-hand instances of people who had been great achievers in the past. These were of significant interest to me because of my own personal desires. It seemed many times as if I was indulging in the aura of walking in history.

Gradually, some of the elements of the structure (or formula) came together, and I was able to test them intensely in the realities of life. When they proved to be workable and sound, I still had to discover some other principles to complete the structure, but I believed I was getting close.

Inspired by the successful launch of my first book in 1984, *How to be Happy Though Rich*, and with the television and other media interest shown around the world, somehow my formula for goal setting all came together.

By 1985, after I had developed, tested, and written down the formula, I shared the manuscript with my friend, Paul J. Meyer, founder and chairman of the board of the Success Motivation Institute Inc., Waco, Texas, USA. He wrote an endorsement for my book and asked me to speak at one of his large international conferences on the subject. He was convinced that my book, *How to Reach Your Life Goals*, would become a classic and still be selling in fifty years's time.

Dr. Robert Schuller also provided a written endorsement for my book and promoted it globally on his famous television program, *Hour of Power*. He made the remarkable statement, "It is the best book ever written on the subject of goal setting." I had to wait another ten years before I was able to put together a sound working model for my book *How to Create Your Own Dynamic Mission Statement that Works*.

Knowing what you want to achieve and the price you are prepared to pay to acquire the desired results continues to evade and confuse most people over a lifetime. The fundamentals may be vague, but you must be convinced that your vision has sufficient value that you are prepared to exchange your life for it.

Over a lifetime, likes and dislikes change with aging, experiences gradually adjust aspirations, and circumstances will bring some changes in your thinking and personality. The process of life will mould and reshape you. In the years ahead, you will become more confident as you learn to handle the harsh challenges that confront you and as you meet various outstanding personalities.

I have found that reading biographies will build into your psyche a vast knowledge of how to overcome incredible odds and will sharpen your understanding of how life shrinks or expands in proportion to the dreams you have and relative to the choices you make. No one can compute the stillborn genius inside you that will never rise above mediocrity if you do not follow through on your commitments. You may continue to dream, but that's like riding an exercise bike—you are using up time and energy, but you are not going to get anywhere! You will soon come to the realization that dreams do not work unless you work at them.

Once you make a commitment, you automatically obtain the power of anticipation and are able to make peace with any bad memories of the past and let them go. The process of goal setting has now become a well-researched and acceptable philosophy for achievement that any serious achiever can use with confidence.

THE GOALS FORMULA

1. Clearly define your goal.
2. Set out your strategy.
3. Plan out the problems.
4. Build in reserves.
5. Relate everything to timeframes.
6. Create a master plan.
7. Action it now.

Clearly Define Your Goal

Describe in clear terms your life goals ... Describe your subordinate major goals ... Describe your subordinate minor goals.

Opportunities are not evenly distributed in the real world, and there is no reserved seat at the banquet table of success set aside for you.

Why not consider a major leadership life goal that can be expanded upon that will magnetize your motivational permanence so that you will fulfil the role that the goal demands? Why a life goal? Because, when you finally expire, everything that you have done in your lifetime is what you have traded your life for, and the cost of a big dream, a small dream, or no dream at all is finally the same. It will cost you your life!

It takes a certain amount of mind sifting to identify desires and face up to the motives that stimulate a person who confidently wears the title "leader." The following questions could act as a guide towards your leadership fulfilment:

- Do you really know what you want to achieve? Can you give an impacting reason why?
- Are there any limiting factors?
- What personnel and material tools do you need to get the job done?
- Do you see any possible exit points?
- How big do you want your goal to be in measurable terms?
- Are there some time partitions of critical importance?
- What specific payments are you prepared to make in terms of time, talent, and treasure?
- Will your goal satisfy your inner yearnings?

- Are you adopting priority economics?
- Are you preparing yourself for the long term?
- Are you creating realistic check points?

In my early years of struggle, I felt the need to channel all my energies through what I called my "Lifetime Code of Conduct," which governs my character and my reaction in all situations. Your most important assets throughout your life will be your family and your character, and both can take years to build and only seconds to destroy.

Set Out Your Strategy

Strategy creates energy ... Strategy saves energy ... Strategy gives direction.

You need to have singleness of thought and purpose to develop the power-drive to activate the law of goal setting. If you desire something for the future, you must plan now. If someone else plans your goals for you, your freedom of choice is violated and your energy and emotional fulfilment reduced. Once you set your life's goals and you know what you want to achieve, the next step is to set out a series of plans to complete the equation.

> **YOU NEED TO HAVE SINGLENESS OF THOUGHT AND PURPOSE TO DEVELOP THE POWER-DRIVE TO ACTIVATE THE LAW OF GOAL SETTING.**

This part of the structure may include making personality changes and educating yourself to develop the necessary competencies to fulfil your desired vision. (In my early days, I spent four years learning words, phrases, basic good manners, and economics.) The famous John D. Rockefeller once said, "I will pay more for the person that can handle people than any other purchasable commodity under heaven."

In my experience, I have observed that a pleasant disposition, tact, and good manners will open doors that money cannot. Within my strategy, it became necessary for me to create twenty-nine supportive goals to build the solid platform I needed if I was going to reach my target. I quickly came to the understanding that hard work alone was insufficient, so instead of becoming a workaholic, I became a "thinkaholic." I often role-played in my imagination how things needed to be done before confirming my next move.

It took me some time to become aware that the strength of my willpower was to become my most powerful force, a force that negated fear and provoked the need to win. It was also important for me to develop a sound reputation and be respected for getting things done.

There needs to be a humanizing of your goal that is achieved by a "mission statement" that "sloganizes" the final destination, the benefits, and the journey in clear, dramatic form that is easy to quote and reliable in content. This will galvanize and excite the crowd into committed action.

During my travels in the USA, I was introduced to a business man in Texas who had built a large organization, turning over many millions of dollars. We spent hours together, and he told me that with all the money that flows through his business, he was barely making a profit. He felt that in the process of all that they had accomplished, there appeared to be blockages and, at times, mismanagement at several levels. I asked him many questions, and the more we talked, it became clear to me exactly what needed to be done. When our conversation came toward a close, he suddenly volunteered the substantial fee that he was prepared to pay if I could solve the problem. I accepted the challenge. We arranged to have breakfast together the next morning, and I was to provide the solution.

I immediately went up to my hotel room, and within thirty minutes, I had written on the hotel stationery what needed to be done. The next morning, I handed a sloganized mission statement to him. To say he was exhilarated would be an understatement! He willingly paid my fee, but I warned him that a second stage was necessary to ensure the success of the plan. But he couldn't wait. He put stage one into immediate effect with spectacular profit returns. I heard sometime later that he went broke. I believe second stage would have prevented that. It was to create a slogan detailing the benefits being offered to the customers in terms of service, quality, and economics, and to have this stamped on every product and all point-of-sale material and advertising.

Plan Out Your Problems

Plans in progress mean power. We will always be surrounded by problems, some of our own making and others that tend to attack us seemingly from no fault of our own. We also have problems that tend to have limited timeframes, and too often we accept as permanent certain problems that are deeply ingrained in our psyche, so they continue to restrict our lives.

I believe we can "plan out our problems." Let me share a number of personal problems that I thought were not changeable and would remain a permanent part of my life, but which I found a way to circumnavigate. I am color-blind, which meant that many business and professional opportunities were closed to me. I am dyslectic, and I did not pass one grade in school. As if that were not enough, I had great difficulty in articulation and mathematics, and I found it was impossible to read music.

Being color-blind later in life did not deter me. I sold paint and ladies' fashions by remembering the numbers of the color codes. I became captain of a large school band by memorizing all the tunes, and I qualified as a licensed real estate valuer, studying by repetition and memorizing the exam material. I completed the four-year course in five months. By painful experience and willpower, I was able overcome my terrible economic way of life by learning without a tutor, and I created my own form of money management with a no-debt philosophy.

I mastered articulation by pronouncing words into a tape-recorder for four years. I must have done a good job, because in New York, I was requested to play on stage in *Hamlet*, and I have often lectured at universities. To become proficient in your areas of weakness, you can observe, read, and study capable leaders. You will discover that all of them seem to thrive on crises and seemingly insurmountable problems, which they exploit to their own advantage.

Build in Reserves

Risk is a normal and necessary part of leadership growth. The saying goes, "The more you insulate yourself against risk, the more you insulate yourself against success." Caution has been the standard for the human race since the beginning of time, but it has never been the measure of a leader.

A leader must face the pressure and the danger of risk and must also shoulder the blame and the consequences of reversals. Nearly fifty years ago, I was invited to work alongside a very successful, wealthy older man who seemed to get along with everyone. He gave me some good advice that has assisted me over many years. We had become involved in a major financial dispute with another business enterprise that had been dishonest over a real estate deal. In the end, we were completely vindicated and financially reimbursed.

My elderly adviser was cordial and forgiving during the process, putting the whole procedure down to an unfortunate error. During the closing discussions, I was about to take them to task, until I saw a slight movement of my elderly associate's hand signaling me to back off. When we left the building, I questioned him about the hand signal, and he said, "Laddie, always let them down gently; you never know if sometime in the future you will need them." (He used to call me "Laddie!") He continued and said, "Never shut the door!"

When we got back to the office, he went on to explain how to build a successful business. He said, "Building a business is just like erecting a tent during a storm. You have to make sure that you hammer the first peg in firmly so that a sudden, unexpected gust of wind cannot dislodge it before you hammer in the next one. Just as you erect the tent, so you build a business. You need to keep checking to make sure that every growth move is secure."

Always seek opportunities to expand your list of helpful relationships and contacts who, over a period of time, become obligated to offer an open door to you, at the very least. I call that "My Friends' Reserve." We all experience times when the going is uphill all the way, and nothing makes sense any more. That is where maintaining a biblical faith is so helpful to sustain your spiritual reserves. I have always endeavored to keep my body fit and get rest before I need it so as to be ready, if necessity requires, for a longer-than-normal work schedule.

Never stop learning, and keep expanding your brain power by studying your craft. To remain directional, keep asking the questions to maintain control, but do not become a wasteful information-gatherer and thereby clutter your mind up with useless trivia. Keep mental reserves. Having physical reserves means taking time off to reflect, and if you are a driven person, you need to take regular time off to allow your body to catch up with your dreams.

Most of the previously mentioned reserves can become unworkable if you do not have sufficient financial reserves. We watch movies and hear stories of people and organizations risking almost everything on the roll of the dice and winning, but there are countless numbers of others that have been mentally and financially crushed because they did not keep sensible, unencumbered, accessible fiscal reserves.

While on a speaking tour in Russia, I was taken out to dinner by two biblical scholars, and during the evening the biblical story of the ten virgins came up. Five were wise and five were foolish. As the evening progressed, the discussion became deeper with several variations and interpretations. I was only half listening and was becoming bored, so I said to my hosts, "You are complicating the story. The principle is simple: If you maintain reserves, you go to the party!" And that principle, if adopted, will permanently change your life. Keep your reserves for setbacks; do not use them for a leap forward, or you may find yourself getting in a deeper hole.

Relate Everything To Timeframes

If you are contemplating some grand scheme for your life, then such a scheme must focus itself upon your life goal to be achievable within a reasonable lifespan. Should your life plan not reasonably fit into the balance of your life, then it must be altered to conform. I am not suggesting that you reduce your life plan, but rather that you examine and revise the plan to allow more to be done in less time.

Now is the time to examine your additional requirements in detail and in practical terms. Evaluate all your timeframes and make allowances for new information. Your programming must allow for delays, earlier-than-expected achievements, and changes in world and local events. It is important to create measurements—timeframes with firmly set dates—for accomplishments in order to prevent a slackening of pace and a reduction in the targets to be met. "Someday" is not a measurement, and hope can be comforting, but it is not a strategy. Firm timeframes with measurements provide a clear and accurate picture of how a job is to be accomplished.

Create a Master Plan

Important as all that I have shared with you is, it must be formulated and blended into a master plan if you are to get the job done. Theories are great and knowledge can be power, but good intentions are only weak promises. Now is the time to tighten all your earlier descriptions. Remove embellishments by measurements and write down your plan in timeslots of five years, ten years, and twenty years. This could be a map for your life, and the time spent on clarifying your plan could save you years of wasted effort and even make your plan expandable. In the process, over time, you will grow into an entirely different person as the clouds of limitation lift and new horizons of growth present a wider picture.

In my earlier years, I found it stimulating at the end of each week to write down an assessment of my efforts and also to review an assessment I had written a year earlier to see where I had exaggerated, lied, or missed the mark. Why not consider creating a workable formula for yourself that will provide an accurate assessment of your daily performance?

6

CREATING A SENSE OF DESTINY

Winston Churchill was undoubtedly one of the greatest orators and crisis political leaders in history. He tells a fascinating story of his childhood impressions. He was with one of his friends, called Evans, and they were talking about what they would do when they grew up. Spontaneously, Churchill announced, "Sometime in the future, Britain will be in great peril, and it will fall to me to save the Empire!"

This statement was supported by a letter he wrote to his mother when he was a young soldier fighting in India. This is how he explained it to her: "I was in the midst of the battle and surrounded by the enemy. I withdrew my revolver and dispatched one of the enemy on my right and then another on my left, and I was as cool then as I am now writing this letter to you. No bullet pierced my tunic, my pony or my person. I believed I was preserved for higher things."

Much later in his life, on the evening he was made Prime Minister of the United Kingdom, as he was preparing for bed, his wife said lovingly to him, "Sweet dreams, my love."

Churchill responded, "Tonight, my dear, facts are more important than dreams! I am walking with destiny." Occasionally, Churchill was deeply depressed; he called depression his "black dog." He would get alone and become unapproachable. During such times, he would rehearse in his mind forthcoming events and how he would deal with them, and eventually he did lead his country to victory.

FOUNDATIONAL PRINCIPALS

If you have reason and desire to attempt to follow a sense of destiny for your life, the following structure may be of help to you:

- The dream
- The vision
- The commitment
- The goal
- The mission
- The destiny

The Dream

"*For a dream comes through much activity, And a fool's voice is known by his many words*" (Ecclesiastes 5:3, NKJV).

At some time in their lives, most human beings have dreamed of doing something great, creating a sense of grandeur towards life. But without a stimulated spirit, there is no dream, and there is nothing as pathetic as a neglected spirit. Without that great force forever urging you on, you will continue to exist in the basement of your life, regretting what could have been.

Regretfully, without action, a dream remains similar to the odyssey of Peter Pan: "Where dreams are born and time is never planned, just think of happy things and your heart will glide on wings to never, never land." We may dismiss the ravings and comments of seemingly talkative fools and scoff at their dreams of grandeur, but in the course of time, people and events can change.

It happened in the lives of people like Martin Luther King Jr., Adolph Hitler, Mahatma Gandhi, John Wesley, John D.

Rockefeller, Winston Churchill, and many others. A dream is usually ignited by a spark deep in the subconscious mind and nurtured through the opportunities and activities of life. Yet without the nourishment of decisive action, it can easily vanish into the ether and be lost forever. To further harness the process of a dream requires an abandonment of fear as you step into the unknown.

Dreaming is not a frivolous waste of time, because when you dream, you are on the periphery of God-likeness, creating something out of nothing. In a sense, you become a mini-creator. Dreaming also illustrates your hidden capacity and your unawakened abilities. There is nothing capricious in God's nature. God will not give you a dream without giving you the ability to fulfil it. But a word of advice: Be careful with whom you share your dreams, or like Joseph, you may find yourself in a pit!

The Vision

"*Then you scare me with dreams and terrify me with visions*" (Job 7:14, ESV).

You are now moving onto an entirely different level of imagination. The clarity and impressions in your mind will start to suggest some strong rearrangements of your thought patterns as you grapple to create some structure to outwork your vision. Illusions of power, responsibility, and confusion will challenge your status quo and haunt you constantly. Mihaly Csikszentmihali, Distinguished Professor of Psychology, puts it this way, "A leader will find it difficult to articulate a coherent vision unless it expresses his core values, his basic identity. One must first embark on the formidable journey of self-discovery in order to create a vision with authentic soul."[3]

---

3 Mihaly Csikszentmihalyi, *Good Business: Leadership, Flow, and the Making of Meaning* (New York, NY: Penguin Books, 2003), 167.

This is where the danger of radical change begins. When the smallest scent of fame or power persists, it can destroy relationships and bring down empires. Unfortunately, many normal, balanced people are overcome by its seductive fragrance. Subconsciously you may experience a disturbing uneasiness as your character is challenged. Your response will teach you that it is easier to keep your character than to repair it.

The Commitment

"*Thou therefore endure hardness, as a good soldier of Jesus Christ*" (2 Timothy 2:3).

When you understand that success has a price, the pain becomes tolerable. In my private discussions with people who want to succeed, I have dealt with physically and intellectually strong men and watched them cower at the thought of the mental pressure of being personally responsible for others in any measurable business or leadership challenge. One great leader said, "I have to be like a sponge and absorb everything that is thrown at me and never flinch!"

The Goal

"*I press toward the goal for the prize of the upward call of God in Christ Jesus*" (Philippians 3:14, NKJV).

You need the dedication to think, plan, and fulfil. While traveling around the world, I meet people who tell me that one of their goals is to visit Australia. If I ask them when, they look at me vaguely and say, "Sometime," but they never make it.

Your goals must be in writing with deadlines for attainment. I am suggesting lifetime goals because:

- there is an element of predictability once you focus your whole life on lifetime goals;
- this will provide motivational permanence; and
- as your capacity expands over time, so does the impact of your goals.

It is interesting that single, expendable life goals are biblically documented. Moses was given a life goal to deliver the people of Israel to the Promised Land, and at the point of delivery, his life was finished and his goal was reached. John the Baptist had a life goal to announce the coming of the long-awaited Messiah, and when the job was completed, his life and goal were finished. Samson had a life goal to be a strong protector of his people, and his life and goal climaxed in final victory. Jesus Christ, the Son of God, the greatest of them all, had a life goal to reconcile all mankind by His sacrificial death and miraculous resurrection.

If despots like Adolph Hitler could conceive the dream of a thousand-year empire, why can't you dream of a hundred-year goal that will be lasting and have the true value called permanence?

The Mission

"*Write the vision and make it plain on tablets that he may run who reads it*" (Habakkuk 2:2, NKJV).

Your objective must be inclusive, clear, and measurable. A mission statement can be described as a written expression of purpose and behavior boundaries worthy of a life's pursuit. It sets a pattern of action that exhibits the character of an organization or person and creates the relationship culture of a person or organization. A mission statement clearly laid out and well presented is a secure anchor in the stormy seas of life. Excellence of character, planning, motivation, and ability draw like-minded people to a cause.

The writings of George Herbert stand as a great lesson to us all. He wrote of a whole empire lost because in his haste, the farrier that was shoeing the horse left off one nail on a horseshoe. The messenger was to ride with the instructions to send more troops immediately to an ensuing battle. "For the want of a nail the shoe was lost, for the want of a shoe the horse was lost, for the want of a horse the rider was lost, for the want of a rider the battle was lost, for the want of a battle the kingdom was lost ... all for the want of a nail!!"

A MISSION STATEMENT CLEARLY LAID OUT AND WELL PRESENTED IS A SECURE ANCHOR IN THE STORMY SEAS OF LIFE.

The mission is the ethics, character, and mechanics of the jsourney in written form. (Re-read "Set out your strategy" in Chapter 5). The tone and nature of the mission description should be like a call to arms and must flow off the tongue or read with dramatic inspirational ease. My mind goes back many years when I was called to reignite a group of 5,000 people to a cause at a prepared meeting in a large hall. I rewrote their mission statement, and with great passion of voice, lighting, and drums, I presented it on stage and was able to strengthen their resolve and create cohesion in a faltering organization.

The Destiny

"*And those he predestined, he also called; those he called, he also justified; those he justified, he also glorified*" (Romans 8:30, NIV).

William Shakespeare in *Hamlet* 5:2 provides an example of a sense of destiny, using the words, "There is a divinity that shapes our ends, rough-hew them how we will." The *Webster Dictionary* describes destiny as "predetermined state or condition foreordained by divine or human will." The *Oxford Dictionary* presents it as "overruling or invincible necessity." The *Macquarie Dictionary* describes it as "the power or agency which determines the course of events." In the reality of life, destiny is explained by different people in many ways.

Alexander the Great called destiny his "hope"; Caesar called it his "luck"; Napoleon called it his "star"; and Dr. Martin Luther King Jr. described it as his "dream." In biblical times, Abraham called it his "promise." To Ezekiel, it was his "prophecy"; for Elijah, it was a "provision"; to Adam and Eve, it was a "punishment"; to the sons of Levi, a "purifier"; for the land of Israel, a "purge"; to Job, a "perseverance"; to Peter, a "proclamation"; to Paul, a "vision"; and to Jesus, as He set his face as flint toward Jerusalem, it was indeed His "destiny."

Over many years, I've read, observed, and studied great people down through the centuries who found it difficult to understand the complexities of a sense of destiny. Most human beings are oblivious of its existence and trade their lives for a lot less than they are worth. In the process, they minimize what they could have been.

There seems to be an invisible thread that magically holds great leaders separate from the rest of humanity. Is it so elusive that it is lost or hides in the cracks of our everyday lives? Questions that will continue to be asked are: How can I obtain it? Where can I find it?

I do not know all of the answers to explain the concept of a personal destiny or calling, but I believe that there are some fundamentals that I have learned and observed through a life of many struggles. I have watched and listened with interest to interviews of famous people on television as they explained their journeys through life. When asked if they would change anything if they were to go back and do it all over again—whether they would make the same mistakes or whether they would change anything—over 95 percent of them said they would repeat the same mistakes and change nothing. On the contrary, I would have liked to change some things, and recalling specifics, I would have done some things better.

Seeking a personal destiny requires mind-searching and trade-offs for a worthy cause. A great deal of trust in your own assessments and judgements can take years to form, or surprisingly sometimes, come magically in moments. The real test for your vision will be in the reality of your personal resolve and the quality and strength of your character.

A great deal of preparatory work is needed to establish the validity and strength of your calling. First, you need to understand the value and power of controlling your own person. Mahatma Gandhi provides us with wonderful guidance in stating seven things that can destroy us:

1. wealth without work;
2. pleasure without conscience;
3. knowledge without character;
4. religion without sacrifice;
5. politics without principle;
6. science without humanity; and
7. business without ethics.

A quote from Agnes de Mille provokes some thought: “No trumpet sounds when the important decisions of our life are made. Destiny is made known silently.”

I believe there are three profound aspects of the destiny challenge that need to inhabit you if you are seeking a sense of destiny to guide your life and control your future. The destiny challenge dares you, drives you, and demands of you.

THE DESTINY CHALLENGE DARES YOU

When the destiny challenge enters the mind, and fantasy falls to the wayside, it dares you. It challenges your status quo and stirs your deepest fears, your moral reticence, and your mental stagnation.

It dares you to be different as you embrace inspirational dissatisfaction. Your boundaries will expand past the still waters of hesitancy and stagnation that for too long remained undisturbed by misplaced hope. It dares you, and even taunts you, to either embrace the challenge or bear a life of shame by living a lie and being a coward. I have met men who didn't respond to the destiny challenge and many years later wept over what their lives could have been.

THE DESTINY CHALLENGE DRIVES YOU

The destiny challenge also drives you and pushes you from comfort to pain, from safety to danger, from words to action, and from indecision to determination. Unable to quench the forceful need, you push beyond your previously known capacity.

It drives you to expand your knowledge, widen your influence, and energize your imagination. It demands your life. You may have to ask yourself the same question that Jacob asked his son, Joseph, when he questioned him, "What is this dream that you have dreamed?" (Genesis 37:10, NKJV)

Many people had a sense of destiny when they were young. You may lie on the sand at the beach on a sunny day or sit by a warm fire on a cold winter's night or gaze into the starry heavens and see a picture of what you are in contrast to what you would like to become.

THE DESTINY CHALLENGE DEMANDS OF YOU

The destiny challenge makes demands of you. It may capture you in a vice-like grip so compelling that it becomes more precious than life itself, and it will require compensation for the fulfilment or the failure of your cause.

It demands every ounce of your energy, every moment of your time, and every fleeting thought, with constancy and obsession until victory is won. The great flame that commenced as a tiny spark and the life that gave its incandescent glow will both finally be extinguished.

A sense of destiny overwhelmingly absorbs an individual's life. We see this in the lives of those who have spent themselves for a cause. Historical legend informs us that Alexander the Great wept when he had no more worlds to conquer. John the Baptist spent his whole life preparing the way for Jesus Christ. Mahatma Gandhi often put his life at risk and defeated the might of the British Empire. General George S. Patton believed that he was created for battle. Paul the apostle gave his life to propagate the Christian faith. Adolph Hitler had such a fixation on his sense of destiny that he promptly disposed of any obstacle. All such persons excluded normal pursuits from their lives in order to follow their sense of destiny, and in some cases, they excluded family and friends as well.

BE ON YOUR GUARD

Unfortunately, under the guise of leadership there are some strangely gifted individuals who possess an aura of invincibility and a hypnotic charisma and who are anxious to lead a cause. With a strong emphasis on noble intent, they lure their followers into a deep commitment with shame and dishonor for opting out.

These so-called leaders have flexible agendas and lack morality. No reason or facts will register against their already concocted agenda, and they ignore any collateral damage they cause. They accept no blame. They expect total obedience and commitment from their followers. They will drain your time, emotions, money, dignity, relationships, and even your very life. They are usually referred to as "out-of-control zealots."

I believe, however, that there is a better way to fulfil your sense of destiny and to manage its grip on your life. I believe you need a Code of Conduct firmly in place to provide balance and to enable you to stand against the tidal waves of seduction that will ultimately surround you as you seek to embrace your destiny challenge. (I have elaborated on this in my book *A Christian Code of Conduct.*)

7

THE FOLLOWERS

There are multiple ways to create support groups. They often commence and work well with a committee of one or with a consultant or chairman of a board of directors, who may suddenly have responsibility for thousands of people!

Here is an example. I wrote a number of self-help books that became very popular, and I received and accepted speaking appointments to large business groups in many countries. The types of businesses were varied, but I was becoming very concerned about the vulnerability of the ordinary moms and dads (called the "down line"), whom I felt were being manipulated and seduced into volunteering by their sponsors (called the "up line"), who were demanding more and more authority over their lives under the promise of financial freedom.

This type of business approach was sweeping the world with enormous success. Inevitably, it became a target for the unscrupulous, and the whole industry became tarred with the same brush. Those who were doing business honestly with their teams and enjoying the results of their modest success had an uplift in their income, and their customers were receiving a good product. However, because many and varied incentives were being offered by start-up breakaway groups that almost overnight were creating extravagant schemes and suspect products, this whole type of business became messy with lawsuits and publicity.

There was such volatility between competing groups that large numbers of participants, including the companies themselves, were on a course of self-destruction, and I had the opportunity to act as a mediator. It was then that my son, Graham, and I wrote a book titled *Global Survey into Multi-Level Marketing* with the subheading *The Rescue of an Industry*. It quickly became the gold standard for assessing the working and reimbursement functions of that type of marketing, which soon became a multi-billion dollar phenomenon.

I was invited to be the lead speaker for many large and diverse international groups, but I would not accept a fee because I believed it could be interpreted as indicating I was on their pay roll, and therefore it could be assumed that I was endorsing their products and their methodology.

My books sold well at functions, and I was approached by a new start-up to become consultant chairman of the board of directors in a non-executive role on a commercial basis, with an offer of shares in the company, which had endorsed the essence of our book. Graham made the arrangement, but I refused the offer of shares, because we did not want to be in a position where even the appearance of compromise could be suspected. I operated successfully in that role for three years as chairman of their board.

I also found it was helpful to keep a private notebook of notations on discussions and week-to-week happenings to keep me up to date and on track. The responsibility was heavy, and I was very aware that all those involved were relying on my ability and reputation.

I was also approached by another substantial group in Europe that was pulling together an international insurance conglomerate. After investigation, I refused on the basis that what they really wanted was to make use of my reputation, which was not for sale.

I have never had any difficulty in obtaining a following. In fact, I receive many emails from people offering to be my personal aid or to work for me free of charge. People ask me, "So what is the secret?" I always respond that there is no secret, it is simply always:

- under-commit and over-perform;
- have an exciting plan;
- act and behave with enthusiastic confidence;
- admit and pay for your mistakes;
- tell the truth to yourself and others;
- paint word pictures of how you see the end results;
- do not surround yourself with minders;
- be available; and
- have a successful track record that is believable and provable.

I have also been involved as chairman of church-related and philanthropic organizations and groups, which are usually run on a democratic basis. You remain in that position as long as you are able to satisfy the majority of those who vote you in, and to do that you must believe absolutely in the cause and have the ability and capacity to settle disputes and maintain progress. (I maintained a position like that for fifteen years.) The one essential of being chairman of a not-for-profit organization is the ability and capacity to raise the finances to keep it afloat.

As an example, I was on the board of a very large international organization. The chairman, who was also president, was undoubtedly one of the most capable I have ever been privileged to have worked with. This man took the organization to heights of effectiveness it had never known in its fifty-year history, and his integrity was impeccable. He had been in that position for ten years and always maintained economic and progressive stability. He held his position only by popular vote.

We were due for the annual board meeting in San Antonio, Texas when we heard that a very nice man who had been in the organization for many years and oozed charisma and charm, but had only modest high-level experience and ability, was being nominated as president and chairman of the board. There were thousands of voters, and it looked as if he was going to win the vote.

The unbelievable happened, and within two hours we had a new president and chairman of the board who had no idea what to do. Within two years, the whole organization fell apart, and it has never recovered.

Being the elected leader of a group with a constitution where majority rules apply can be likened to walking on a tightrope, as opinions and focuses change, depending on those with the loudest or most persuasive voices and the moods of the people. As an elected leader, you will be faced with the task of keeping the peace and staying and improving things, in accord with the confines and targets of general agreement. The struggles usually come at the annual convention when all facets of the organization express multiple conflicting ideas and opinions, sometimes with much vigor and emotion. The way to quiet down the proceedings and seek to obtain order and consensus is to break the meeting up into cell groups of like-minded people to clarify their case for growth or change. After the given time for this, the large group comes together with each cell group having chosen their presenter to make their case and allow time for questions. Ensure all are heard.

Of course, each group expects their submission to be accepted and implemented. This is generally an impossibility, but the process must be seen to be fair. When all the submissions have been made and questions asked and answered, it can be complicated and seem cold-hearted in a democratically run institution not to offer a process for evaluation and selection for action in an open forum. I have faced this many times over a number of years and been lobbied well into the night by those who were trying to get me to take sides or make a recommendation, either of which would be improper.

The way I always managed the situation was to put a color code or an identification mark for each submission on a large board and relate to all with voting capacity and explain the process: "We have before us on the board all acceptable representations that require a vote for your approval and subsequent action. Everyone has the opportunity to have one vote to determine the first, second, and third most popular choices, and the remainder are to be noted in the minutes for future possibilities." Some people will be disappointed that their submission was not chosen and they may even leave the organization, but no one can accuse the selection of being unfair or rigged.

I have also been on boards of directors of non-profit organizations, both local and international, where the founder is president and has total authority. This has worked wonderfully well under a three-tier system where the founder is ex officio on all boards and committees. Let me explain.

Probably the most important board is the Finance and Planning board. This is where the founder expresses the vision, and the board members assist with the basics of the plans and help raise the finance. Each member on this board must have their own successful business and invest financially in cash to support the work. The founder must always be on the front-line of continued fund-raising. The board members have no authority over staff. They must not retain copies of minutes, and at the end of each year they vacate their positions and may be re-elected if required. This allows for the release of some board members who have proven to be ineffective or wish to retire. It also creates opportunity for new blood. No staff members are permitted on this board, which would probably meet monthly. It can be a good idea for the board members to meet with their spouses and special guests for a friendly social evening for lobbying.

The next board is an Advisory board, which would only meet quarterly. Its members need specialized expertise and third-person influence. They can be called on for outside advice and to provide valuable information, fund-raising, and other contacts. The third board of directors would be the Ethics group, making sure that the organization does not stray from its original foundations and raison d'être. Every six months, this board would examine the progress, expenditure, and future plans in relation to the desired direction and outcome.

I have often been asked, "What is your gift?" The answer is simply this: "I get things done." I admit that I am something of a loner and I prefer to do things my way. Many people would like to partner with me, but in the long run I end up having to carry them. This just slows down the ride, as they become baggage. If I agree to do something, then leave me alone and go home to bed, and I will get the job done. If it is outside my expertise, I will find the right person for the job, or if there needs to be a crowd, I will create one.

Once someone thought they could get me involved by appealing to my wife to persuade me to attend a retreat. She responded, "If you use the word 'retreat' in front of my husband, you will never get him to first base." Another time when I was responding to some questions at a meeting, the two men in front of my wife agreed in their discussion that I would be tough! My wife, Robina, tapped them on their shoulder and said, "I am his wife, and you are right! He is tough! But only on himself!"

If you have difficulty getting a crowd, why not rent a crowd? It is easy. Just work out what you need them for, create a simple event, and invite several separate groups. By a few personal visits, find out what their "hot button" is, and create an event that would interest them. I did it once, and with only $1,000, had a feature opportunity to speak to over 40,000 people. At a youth happening I persuaded the wood chipboard industry to donate their rejects, and then convinced a transport company to transport them to a location that was allotted at no cost to a country fair. We transformed them into a "Star Wars" maze, and then asked Coca Cola for some cartons of drinks. This was a great drawcard for the young people who went through it, and it was expressly built to teach some wholesome lessons on life. We ran out of cool drinks in fifteen minutes and stopped counting bodies after 42,000! It was a sensational success.

Crowds are not a miracle. Crowds are a great idea. They require good planning, excellent execution, and hard work, but what the crowd receives—and how the crowd responds—are the pay off.

If you are aspiring to great leadership, you will be on a useless merry-go-round if all you are going to do is to look for an existing group you can fit into and finally work your way up to the leadership level. Having empires in your mind and feeling the compulsion of greatness has to be nurtured in graduated steps. As I look back over a long life, I focus on those with whom I have spent time and who seemed to tick all the boxes for achievement and greatness, but who have not yet made the courageous step out of their own fear-imposed restrictions. They did all the studies, worked on growing their contact base, critiqued the action of others, wrote great submissions, and volunteered many ideas. These people

> **HAVING EMPIRES IN YOUR MIND AND FEELING THE COMPULSION OF GREATNESS HAS TO BE NURTURED IN GRADUATED STEPS.**

became a cheer squad for those on the front line and said they were waiting for the great opportunity to emerge. Some of them I coaxed for twenty years, believing that they were genuinely seeking to make a mark of some significance, but suddenly when the time for action came, they missed the opportunity.

I finally made up my mind that I was going to establish something that one of them claimed he was prepared to trade his life for. He spent hours with me, eloquently expressing his life's dream, and we documented it precisely. I then set about calling on favors with my international contacts to set up a scenario that opened doors for him, far beyond what he could have arranged for himself. All he had to do was accept, and with no restrictions, step into the global yearnings of his dreams. When I presented this to him, he agreed it would be his life's dream come true and would address every facet and more of what he wanted for nearly thirty years. He was now faced with the reality of it all. This man that I had known for so many years, assisted with countless meetings, and listened to over many hours, stood before me and said, "I will have to seek some advice. Please give me several days to consider." The end result was that his advisers told him the offer was too big, and he agreed with them.

Many of my boyhood friends and the business acquaintances I have had over my lifetime have unfortunately aborted their dreams on the altar of fear and neglect. They call me from time to time to talk over old times and lift their spirits. Those whom I have in some way helped in the past with advice and encouragement call, send gifts, and even make long journeys just to say "thank you."

The type of leadership that seems to suit me best and brings out all of my gifts, attention, and abilities is when I understand that something needs to be done and I decide to do it. I make my expected objective clear, undertake my own planning, and accept full responsibility for its cost and its fulfilment or failure. I share my plans and expectations with some notable and important people and request the use of their names as a board of reference.

In case they have any doubt about my ability to perform, I select volunteers personally, explain their role in detail, and get them to agree to a "no let-out" clause: "You start and you finish." I set the rules, and I am the only one they are accountable to. Sounds tough, but it works if you know how to measure and treat people right and they trust you.

With just twelve volunteers, we were able to fly a music group in from Nashville and a lead country western singer from Kentucky, build and train two back-up choirs, and put on forty-two crowded concerts. We brought from Indonesia an expert trainer in counseling, who trained over a thousand people in the course of several meetings.

When the whole event was completed, I cannot recall one single conflict among the volunteers, and everyone involved made it quite clear to me that they would be available again any time in the future. True to my word, all accounts were paid. I finished up completely exhausted, but with everyone well satisfied. We need to acknowledge the masses.

There are some simple ways to be a good follower. Here are some key points to remember:

- Your presence counts, because without words you have signified interest and support. If you cease to attend, it follows that your interest has not been stirred. If your interest has been stirred and you want to participate, there are also other ways to show support, such as talking to others in an approving way and pointing out what the program is endeavoring to achieve. A donation of any kind is always appreciated and attention-getting.

- Ask if you can help. Because there is so much to do even in the smallest organization, a genuine helper of seeming insignificance can be a treasure. I recall one man who had limited abilities but possessed a sense of responsibility and a happy disposition. Smith offered to do anything if he could be involved. The only thing it was felt he could handle was to watch over the automobiles in a large park and pick up the papers, which he did tirelessly in all weather and at all hours. Nobody knew when Smithy passed away until junk piled up in the car park and cars were being broken into. It took a well-attended funeral and a large crowd of mourners to show final gratitude. Do what you can and be part of the parade.
- Withhold your criticism. If you get to the point that you are fed up, having aired your grievances and found no one is interested and you can't live with it anymore, then leave! Quietly, with dignity, and do not sabotage.
- If you want to get some recognition and possible promotion to a higher level, arrive early, leave late, and clean up everyone else's mess. If you want to take it a bit further, put an obvious suggestion on the leader's desk and wait for him or her to contact you.
- If you are getting restless and are starting to feel the energetic pull of inspirational dissatisfaction, then it is possible you may be receiving an inward call to leadership. If this is what you believe to be the situation, then you should leave with good feelings shared by all. Never close the door. The needs of today may not be the needs of tomorrow.

As you walk into my private study, your eyes will eventually come in contact with a sign that says: "Lead, follow, or get out of the way." Seems abrupt, forceful, and even a little bit arrogant, but for someone who has a cause and is prepared to trade their life for it, it becomes a strong and urgent battle cry.

Those who do not have the urgency and the commitment to personally blaze a trail toward a magnificent obsession are often the very people who were once enthused and at the very least still want to follow and be part of the parade. In the heart of every human being is a longing to be appreciated and share in the adventure of being a part of some significant happening in their lifetime. By being a part of it, they are entitled to share in its glory.

Once a year I used to get a phone call from a very old man whom I call Mr. T. He had a major but unseen part of a significant happening thirty years earlier. We would settle into lunch together, and I would stimulate him to recall what took place so many years ago. His face would light up as he went through the details of setbacks and problems they had to overcome to realize the final glorious success of a great event. The recollection brought tears to his eyes. Nobody remembers his name or recognized his deep involvement, yet here he was sitting next to me bursting with gratitude and humble pride that he played his part in such a great occasion, which had made a very positive impact on the lives of thousands of people.

Mr. T. would walk back to his automobile with a strong gait, seeming to me to look a little taller. I stood there smiling as he departed, knowing that the same time next year I would receive a phone call for lunch when we would recall the event of many years ago and when I would thank him again. It was that event that had changed my life.

We stand in awe of the greats of the now and the greats of the past, who will remain in history and be admired by many in antiquity. The many who were used as cannon fodder in battle, and those who, without complaint, tirelessly filled the ranks in war and in peace. Today, there are followers who are still seeking leaders who possess virtue, vigilance, and wisdom. The masses of people in many nations would accept that they are just average human beings— nothing special, just average. They vote for politicians on polling days and go to average jobs. They do average things around their house and pay the average mortgage. These people buy their average groceries at the local supermarket and are served by average people.

The average person does not understand or even care about great thoughts like Albert Einstein's theory of relativity or quantum physics, and is unlikely to understand the complexities of world market economies or the need to probe into outer space. Average people just plod on day-by-day, week-by-week, trying to make ends meet. And in the process of life, they look after their families by taking their kids to and from school and holding their marriages together. They get some excitement and entertainment occasionally, watching football or going to the movies, but most of the time they feel unimportant, insignificant, and unappreciated.

Mr. and Mrs. Average look with unknowing eyes at those who seem effortlessly to forge ahead, and at times they wonder where they might have gone wrong and missed out on the lucky breaks. Many Christians go to church but struggle to live out their faith in a meaningful way and occasionally ask themselves, "Is it really all worth it? Does it make any difference?" Amazingly, they continue with the bored feeling that they are just support fodder for all that is happening around them. The masses of these unnumbered people continue unaware of the crucial role that they play in the kaleidoscope of events that surround them constantly. They do not realize that their continued vitality is the strong link in the stability of all national and global security.

Without the daily routine of the average masses, governments would collapse and communication would fail; banks would have no money, stores would have no produce, and great factories and machinery would become rusty, useless junk. Without Mr. and Mrs. Average, we would have no one to clean our hospitals and run our transportation services, and the wealthy would become impoverished. Mr. and Mrs. Average are the heroes in war and peace. Our politicians only recognize them when they want their vote, and forget them once they are elected. Then they create complicated, unjust laws to control and restrict Mr. and Mrs. Average for the mysterious inexplicable "common good," and are surprised with the distrust shown to them.

The horrors of the French Revolution were avoided in Great Britain (according to Leckey, an Irish historian) by the preaching of John Wesley, which stirred the conscience of the ruling class, but the Russian Revolution exploded into a bloodbath of tyranny and dictatorship, enslaving the lives of millions under Communist rule.

Leaders and aspiring leaders continue in their manipulative ways of knowingly confusing people and ignoring the need for a Citizens's Code of Conduct. Such a Code of Conduct should not be restricted to talent and virtue, but should embody the individual responsibility of citizens for their own well-being and ensure generous, collective protection for those who are mentally or physically handicapped.

We must not take the people for granted.

8

A LEADERLESS WORLD AT WAR WITH ITSELF

The expectations for the beginnings of a brave new world in the twenty-first century remain trampled as dry dust under the carpet of leadership make-believe and sloppy, meaningless platitudes. The great philosophical sayings of the past have long since vaporized into a misty, grey cloud of irrelevance where no moral compass exists. The world cries out for equality on the basis of what they receive without any consideration of personal gifting, positioning, or effort.

Martin Luther King Jr. urged us all to make personal judgements for mankind on the basis of character. He believed that whatever your status, gender, race, or pursuits, you are entitled to respect and acceptance relative to the quality of your character.

Thomas Jefferson's view gives a somewhat different perspective and considers "virtue and talent." By the word "virtue," he means manners and character. He says that "talent" can be gifted or developed.

The economist and sociologist Vilfredo Pareto developed the "Principle of Imbalance" in his Eighty-Twenty Rule. He claims that 80 percent of the wealth of a nation's production, influence, and skills are produced by 20 percent of the people.

Somehow and in some way, each of these three illustrations are correct, but things become blurred and complicated when it comes down to individual reasoning, especially for those who are ambitious.

It is time for existing and potential leaders to rethink the past, with all its errors and fanciful promises of prosperity and growth, and start with a clean slate. Democracy and the republic, in their present form, are already beginning to destroy themselves from within by turning our populations into weak, demanding dependants, instead of strong, self-reliant citizens. The strength, inward care, and solidarity of the family unit is now relegated to a different era that lacked the birth control pill or the welfare system.

Most political leaders seem to bypass the obvious. They reward people with concessions when they allow themselves to develop preventable illnesses, and continually rescue people and organizations from financial difficulties created by their own bad habits and lack of personal discipline. This only amplifies the problem. In simple terms, our governments should encourage the good and discourage the bad. They should expect people to abide by a simple Citizens's Code of Conduct, which would benefit all people and be in the interests of all political persuasions.

The Western world's short-term view means that political parties continue to try and out-bid their opponents in a dangerous war of auctioning off goodies to voters in order to get elected into office. The requirements to run for office are faulty and are usually based on flimsy, massaged criteria that do not examine knowledge of the country's Constitution or personal behavior or fiscal abilities. Political contenders make careless promises without inbuilt, enforceable time-frames or consequences.

It has almost reached the point that the largest single voting bloc in democratic countries are those on the government's pay roll, and they will always vote in favor of job security. We all want a government that is benevolent and fair and treats all equally, hoping that one size fits all, but in reality, the opposite occurs.

Two people can grow up in the same family with equal education and opportunities, yet their lives and fortunes become total opposites. One will strive to do the best possible, and the other may choose to take things as they come. The first one works long hours to build a business, supplies jobs, and becomes wealthy. Both are now treated differently by the same government, even though they breathe the same amount of air and use the same roads, water, street lights, and sewerage. The one who worked hard is now penalized with higher taxes and has no possibility of receiving an old-age pension unless he spends all his money and becomes broke. He is even vilified by some sectors of society. This is where the Pareto Principle of Imbalance is proven: 20 percent of the population pays 80 percent of the bills.

The nations that will sustain growth in the future will be those that demonstrate and appreciate those who honestly create jobs and wealth. John Paul Getty (once reported to be one of the richest men in the world) once said, "If all the money and property of the world were divided up equally at say three o'clock in the afternoon, by 3.30 p.m. there would already be notable differences in the financial conditions of the recipients. Within that first thirty minutes, some adults would have lost their share. Some would have gambled theirs away, and some would have been swindled or cheated out of their portion (thereby making some others richer). The disparity would increase with growing momentum as time went on. After ninety days, the difference would be staggering. And, I am

THE NATIONS THAT WILL SUSTAIN GROWTH IN THE FUTURE WILL BE THOSE THAT DEMONSTRATE AND APPRECIATE THOSE WHO HONESTLY CREATE JOBS AND WEALTH.

willing to wager that, within a year or two at the most, the distribution of wealth would conform to patterns almost identical with those that previously prevailed."[4]

It is impossible to even legislate permanent equality when each person has their own wants, desires, and expectations. We have forgotten the great economic recessions of the past, and in so doing, have repeated on a much larger scale the very actions that created them. The world appears to be at war with itself, and the billions in money, aid, and personnel that have been sent to places like Africa over the last 150 years have not curtailed the killing and starvation that persists daily. The conflicts in the Middle East are now compounded by religious hatred and intolerance and are expanding through terrorism to other parts of the world. Some parts of Europe after World War II were almost obliterated, but conflicts over ancient lands still persist. Nations which for decades have had the title of "third world" are waiting to be bailed out of their low status without being able or prepared to adapt their culture and create and stick to an effective Constitution that will lift them out of poverty.

You may be reading this book hoping to find answers regarding your own leadership interests and concerns for the present and also looking towards the future. It may not be too late for us to stop the slide towards our social, economic, and moral oblivion if we are prepared to act now. If change is to take place, it must start with the individual's active value system, but that alone will not make a good leader. I have witnessed throughout my lifetime more harm and distress caused by honest fools than by capable crooks.

We all want strong morality in leaders, but they must also possess other attributes, such as activity, knowledge, wisdom, people skills, willpower, and prodigious energy, to name just a

---

4 http://www.quoteswise.com/john-paul-getty-quotes.html

few. Although leaders have great magnetism, they are generally smart enough to realize that they are created and sustained by their followers. At times, decisions have to be made between two evils in order to protect the people. You may have to choose the lesser of two evils, knowing full well that it is the only way to go. Then you are confronted with the dichotomy, knowing you have to make a bad choice to put things right. That is when a strange kind of moral courage is required. The leader must accept the blame and accusations when the decision backfires, and give the credit to the followers when it becomes beneficial.

When Lee Iacocca became president of Chrysler Motors, it was collapsing, and he cut thousands of jobs. He then sold off anything that they could do without. He radically changed the whole management structure of the company and made it profitable. When asked later if he'd made mistakes, he admitted that in his haste he had to fire a large number of good people to save the jobs of others. I was to have had breakfast with him one morning in Southern California, but it did not work out. However, I understand he was still hurting over the people he had to make redundant and the effect on their families.

In some countries, the culture and even the religion make hard decisions quite matter of fact. If, for instance, in a particular country you were in a boat with your wife and your mother, and the boat began to sink and you could only save one, who would you save? To some the answer is obvious—you choose your mother, because you cannot replace your mother, but you can replace your wife!

If we were to state what we believe would be the requirements of an acceptable leader, we might specify the following:

- We would like our leaders to have the personality and physical features that display presence and bearing, a good command of language, and a strong resonant voice (their public image).

- The way they respond with clever remarks in spontaneous and staged interviews always gets a thumbs-up with the public.
- If leaders can at any time gain the moral high ground over a contentious issue, that would accelerate their crowd approval.
- It is essential that they have the ability to formulate and articulate a believable plan of possible benefits.
- Leaders need to be sensitive to and understanding of followers' motives and needs (and vice versa).

During a crisis situation in a city, a concerned group of citizens met in a hall to discuss and prepare a plan to choose a leader. The group found it difficult to make a choice until well into the meeting when someone who was late because of searching for a parking spot was immediately nominated, seconded, and elected as leader. All this took place before this person could object or reach a chair to sit on. Known as a family person of virtue and talent, the person accepted the challenge and helped lead the group towards a successful outcome. But it does not always work that way. We usually make a choice on availability and settle for less than is needed because ability is usually unavailable.

Sometimes a leader automatically evolves and fills a space. Those who set a good example by their lifestyle, speak encouragement to the good, and are prepared to speak up against the bad, become candidates. We all like to think that if we had a choice of the qualities we wanted in our leader, we would place morality and fairness high on the list. But only in the immediate moment of being faced with a major complex decision, knowing that all options are equally bad and that delay is not a safety net, will you fully understand the heavy burden of leadership.

At these times, the steadfastness of your courage and character will be your only fortress, and in the future your conscience will be your comforter or accuser. Saint Augustine said, "A weakened sense of responsibility does not weaken the fact of responsibility."

I was in Russia with my wife when we saw a man dressed up impersonating Joseph Stalin. I was watching him walking down the street in his military uniform. It became interesting as some people ran up and kissed him while others clapped their hands and cheered. I was surprised when still others booed, shook their heads, turned their backs on him, and walked away.

My inquiry into the reason for the different reactions provided a reasonable answer. The ones who embraced and cheered him said, "We were poor as Communists under Stalin, but we were secure and were able to cope." The group that walked away said, "Stalin curtailed our freedom and gave us no incentive to build a better life." One man told me a story about Joseph Stalin's harsh leadership methods of maintaining control and claimed it was true. When Marshall Stalin was responding to a suggestion that because of his harshness he would finally lose his hold over the Russian people, he walked calmly out to where some chickens were scratching the hard earth trying to find something to eat. He then took a big stick and started to beat the chickens and scatter them, and then he waited a few minutes and threw some wheat on the ground and they came running back. He smiled and said to his critic, "It works with people too."

With growth or crises, all organizations and governments either have to adapt to change when it is needed, or perish. If they are unable or unwilling to do so, everyone loses.

Leaders usually have to act on what they perceive to be hard facts, and they really do understand the uncomfortable outcome that some of the followers have to endure. This can become a heavy burden for them to bear and can plague them for a lifetime. Should you desire to become a leader and be seeking a beginning or a move upward from your present status, you may find help or solace in following the tested graduated steps that I either chose or fell into over a lifetime.

Beware that the full shock waves and the exhilarating elation, hurt, and ingratitude that leaders experience can never be fully explained or emotionally expressed in mere words. If leadership is your choice or your over-bearing sacrificial calling, then bear it bravely, or abdicate now before it fastens you in its grip.

MY FINAL ADVICE

Many are equipped to take hold of the leadership baton but do not see the need or are unwilling to trade their life for the uncertainties it presents. Leadership is a lifetime pursuit that has no start or finish times. It will stretch your visionary, mental, and physical boundaries to the limit and then demand more. It is a life traded for a group of people or a cause. Your identity is intertwined within it, and most times it is inescapable.

Your fear will threaten all your human qualities as you consider, commence, and continue in leadership. The measure of its extent and the direction it flows will, to a large extent, dictate the end result. This fear is real and intimidates the mind and emotions. It relates to your time, physical, and financial circumstances, limitations, reputation, and all sorts of variables in the present and future. It becomes a blockage and has manipulative reasoning power that can justify almost anything and cover or reject any multitude of defences. Your fear threshold, if not increased, will finally put a limit on your achievements. Do not lightly brush aside the very real power of fear to restrict your leadership capacity.

Your indispensable protective asset is to create a Lifetime Code of Conduct. Once formulated, it will become an important part of your everyday activity. Good decisions will be made much more easily with uncompromising predictability and will provide your followers with a real sense of security. Having a Code of Conduct will also minimize conflict within the ranks and keep your team focused, and it will draw like minds toward you.

WHERE ARE THE LEADERS?

Where are the leaders?
You well might ask as you travel here and there.
Are they hiding, dead, or nowhere to be found?
Are there none who care that the need is great, the cause is true,
the battle line is drawn?
Who will be our champion?
We call. But none come to the fore.
Are we to perish distraught, put down, and never more to rise?
Is there not just one who will answer to the cries?
I sought from east to west, and from north to south,
To try and find a soldier brave to answer to the shout.
Perhaps a bugle call will rouse, the red blood in his veins.
Come quickly bugler, sound, before it's all in vain.
The danger presses closer, at every halting breath.
Arise and lead please, somebody!
Before there's nothing left.
But not a murmur do I hear, when listening for a call.
It seems as if it might be me, a leader after all.
Then I'll do my best, I'll lead the rest.
To any danger I will go.
With muscles tense and iron will, to charge against the foe.
With victory within sight, the enemy will flee.
And no one knew until that hour, the leader could be you or me!

Destiny of the 3rd Millennium
US$2,500.00
www.wces.vu/store

As a personal tutorial Destiny has no equal, and has been applauded globally for its practicality and results in the fields of entrepreneurship, personal development, and leadership.

During the 10 hours of instruction in DVD and CD format you will discover the principles of time management, economic security, goal setting, will power, crisis management, directional thinking, how to lead, ideas that make money, motivational permanence, decision making, how to create a heritage, how to handle stress, how to create and control a board of directors, how to build a mission statement that works, how to discover your sense of destiny and much more.

The information contained in this program is clearly understandable and immediately usable.

www.ingramcontent.com/pod-product-compliance
Lightning Source LLC
Chambersburg PA
CBHW030635300826
50290CB00010B/138/J
9781486615490